to Geraldine Ann Foote

COLOR IN PUBLIC SPACES:
Toward a Communication-Based Theory
of the Urban Built Environment

by

Kenneth E. Foote

THE UNIVERSITY OF CHICAGO
DEPARTMENT OF GEOGRAPHY
RESEARCH PAPER NO. 205

1983

Copyright 1983 by Kenneth E. Foote
Published 1983 by the Department of Geography
The University of Chicago, Chicago, Illinois

Library of Congress Cataloging in Publication Data

Foote, Kenneth E., 1955–
  Color in public spaces.

  (Research paper/The University of Chicago, Department of Geography: no. 205)

  Includes bibliographies: p. 143.

  1. Color in architecture. 2. Visual communication. 3. Color—Psychological aspects. I. Title. II. Series: Research paper (University of Chicago. Dept. of Geography); no. 205.
H31.C514 no. 205 [NA2795] 910s [729] 83-5809
ISBN 0-89065-111-6

Research Papers are available from:

The University of Chicago
Department of Geography
5828 S. University Avenue
Chicago, Illinois 60637
Price: $8.00; $6.00 series subscription

TABLE OF CONTENTS

LIST OF ILLUSTRATIONS

LIST OF TABLES

PREFACE

The principal preoccupations of this monograph are the urban
built environment--the landscape of brick, stone, wood, and mortar
that comprise the physical city and stand as an important aspect of
the human urban experience--and its analysis by means of a broadened
conception of human communication. The first of these
preoccupations has been the inspiration for a large literature
concerned with the relation between material, architectural, and
architectonic artifacts and the social dynamics of the culture
within which they are found. This study, as an elaboration or new
departure, suggests that this relation can be effectively conceived
as one of communication. The analysis of color in public spaces is
introduced as an example of how this conception can be developed
with reference to empirical observation. Once color acts out this
supportive role its analysis is pursued no further.

This is not to deny that color as found in the cityscape is an
interesting and tempting topic worthy of an encompassing historical
and cross-cultural analysis; this study hopes to make some small
contribution in this direction. Nevertheless during my research I
often had to remind myself that my findings were intended primarily
for an audience interested in the physical city, as opposed to one
principally alert to color. Because the interests and methods of
these two audiences diverge it seemed ill-advised to wander too far
from my original preoccupations so as perhaps to trespass into the
iconography of color phenomena. More importantly, I felt that to
delve more deeply into color might distract the reader from
comparing this study's conception of the built environment to its
contemporaries, and it is in this connection that the contribution
of this monograph may be most timely.

For years scholars from a number of fields have been been
converging, I feel, on an interpretation of the sort outlined in the
following chapters. The genre of research concerned with the "city
as symbol," that is the symbolic import of urban physical
morphology, now overlaps the literature of semiotics. Research
stemming from environmental psychology and behavioral geography can
now be connected with that arising from the study of non-verbal
communication. Linguistic theory, at least in some circles, is
being "contextualized" in accordance with models of communication
which stress empirical observation of human action rather than the
logicality and truth-value of abstract grammars. Sociolinguists and

students of material culture are coming to new and interesting
conclusions concerning the relation of language, costume, and the
commonplace objects of everyday life to characteristics of social
form. Perhaps I am naive to believe that these developments are
complementary or will fit together neatly enough to presage a vital
future for the type of research advocated in this monograph. My
optimism may obscure my view of other dominant trends in these
literatures which will preclude their further convergence.

Still, I hope that my surmise proves correct, that these
ideas of independent disciplinary origin are approaching the point
of convergence. Even if my forecast is wrong, the state of
contemporary thought seems to portend, at the very least, a period
of fruitful development. By breaking some restrictive assumptive
bonds and violating some traditional disciplinary boundaries it may
be possible to link the form of large-scale cultural artifacts to
certain intrinsic properties of human thought processes so as to
ground our understanding of the physical city, the very structure of
the urban built environment, on fundamental features of human
action, interaction, and communication. I can only hope that this
monograph will help support the construction of such an
understanding rather than damage the present, necessary scaffolding
as a useless incendiary.

ACKNOWLEDGMENTS

This monograph addresses a number of questions concerning urban form, architecture, and culture which originally drew me to the discipline of geography, into graduate study, and eventually to the research project presented here. I am indebted to the many people who helped me formulate these questions and directed me in the search for their answers within traditions of geographic and cultural inquiry.

At the University of Wisconsin the creative atmosphere present in the Department of Geography allowed me as an undergraduate readily to perceive Geography's interdisciplinary scope and stimulated a curiosity concerning questions of multidisciplinary compass. The advise of David Ward, Clarence Olmstead, and especially Robert Sack--whose guidance and encouragement continued beyond my term of study in Madison--was appreciated.

During graduate study at the University of Chicago I came under the tutelage of three very fine advisors. Paul Wheatley, in providing the overall intellectual guidance for my studies, stimulated my curiosity and guided me to sources at the far reaches of social theory and research. His erudition and insight defined the terms of a challenging apprenticeship. Victor Yngve's contribution to my studies extends beyond the specific citations found in the following pages. At a time when I was doubtful of reconciling the precepts of linguistic, semiotic, and communication-based theory with regard to the analysis of the urban built environment, Mr. Yngve convinced me that the problems I had intuited were genuine, but nonetheless surmountable. I am also indebted to William Pattison. Without his involvement this project could not have been completed. His keen understanding of my intellectual background, inclinations, and progress coupled with a vital commitment to education and teaching were an essential part of my years of graduate study.

I would like to thank many other people who either helped me to articulate the ideas that are addressed here (sometimes long ago) or were kind enough to read and comment upon preliminary drafts of this monograph. These benefactors include Dan Bluestone, Carol Hendrickson, Benjamin Lee, Robert Sack, Milton Singer, and Victor Turner. The writings of Paul Feyerabend, Clifford Geertz, Erving Goffman, William Labov, Bronislaw Malinowski, I.A. Richards, George Simmel, Stephen Toulmin, Thorstein Veblen, and Max Weber have been of great value. I gratefully acknowledge financial support in the manner of fellowships awarded me by the Department of Geography and Division of Social Sciences at the University of Chicago (1976-1977) and the National Science Foundation (1977-1979,1980-1981). Also, because this is the first Research Paper to have progressed from first draft to final camera-ready copy by way of the University of Chicago's computer text-formatting and printing facilities, special thanks must be extended to Bernie Lalor, Joel Mambretti, and Charles Hodge for support and much extra work on my behalf.

For personal support during the writing of this monograph I wish to thank Susan Lester, my parents, as well as my brothers and their families. Finally, a special debt is owed to the many musicians with whom I have had the good fortune to rehearse and perform over many years in a wide variety of settings. Their devotion to music of so many idioms--especially that of the Middle Ages, Renaissance, and early Baroque--provided relaxing and inspiring counterpoint to the strains of work and study.

The Memorial Union
Madison, Wisconsin
December, 1982

CHAPTER I

COLOR IN PUBLIC SPACES AS A PROBLEM OF INTERPRETATION

Introduction

The experience of color is a primary feature of urban life. We cannot avoid its impress, especially in urban public spaces where so much social activity takes place. Regardless of a city's size or the culture and era within which it is found, color is always woven into the physical fabric of the city. The individual buildings and objects from which cities are constructed are saturated with color, no matter how drab and commonplace these colors may seem to habituated city dwellers.

So pervasive is the experience that we must often overcome a certain perceptual satiation before we are able to recognize the regularities and patterns of its use. In cities of the Western world urban public spaces include systems of uniformly colored streets which are highlighted by a regular and vivid pattern of traffic and information signs. The buildings and structures which border and give definition to public space seem to be colored in relation to their uses. Color permeates our experiences in cities right down to the point where every building, almost every organization differentiates itself from its neighbors on the basis of a change of color. This continues in private as well as public, and as we move from exterior to interior spaces. Yet how meaningful are the colors which are infused into the surfaces of cities everywhere?

Given the salience of color as an attribute of the physical city, it is perhaps surprising that little attention has been given to answering this question. It has been addressed, if only partially, in a number of ways: the part color plays in the architectural design process, the canons which have governed the application of color to public and religious buildings through time and cross-culturally, and in relation to questions of the psychology of perception or of the imageability of physical forms.[1] Yet even

---

1. Many scholars have discussed color use in relation to the architectural design process and as it pertains to the psychology of color perception including

1

with the resulting information available to us, our curiosity is not completely satisfied. The fact remains that if we accept color in the cityscape as an interesting topic of study, one worthy of attention in its own right, we are at a loss for theories capable of relating it to the people and societies which make use of it.

Although this may seem to be a small oversight color is anything but a minor part of a great whole: the physical city. The physical form of cities in itself demands more study for it is related to almost all activities urban dwellers engage in. It is a home, a habitat, almost a stage upon which roles and lives are acted out, and behind which are built new sets and props for future productions. Color is very much related to this action. If our theories concerning this built environment cannot adequately encompass color, are they of any real value for understanding of the physical city generally?

As an attribute of the physical city color is inextricably linked to questions of culture and social forces in their relation to material expression. These general questions have spurred the development of social and cultural theory for decades and centuries, it should not be surprising to discover some earlier models for the understanding of both the physical city and color use found within it. There are a number of interpretations available to us which relate socio-cultural process to color. The major ones revolve around psychological theories and perceptual archetypes, semiotic models which view physical form and color use as part of a system of meaningful signs and symbols, and the extension of linguistic analogies into the domain of physical forms so that color is seen as a language with its own grammar and syntax.

Anna Campbell Bliss, "Color Selection as a Design Decision," *American Institute of Architects Journal* 67 (October 1978):60-65; Nory Miller, "The Re-Emergence of Color as a Design Tool," *American Institute of Architects Journal* 67 (October 1978):40-55; Faber Birren, *Color, Form, and Space* (New York: Reinhold Publishing Co., 1961) and *Color and Human Response* (New York: Van Nostrand Reinhold, 1978); Waldron Faulkner, *Architecture and Color* (New York: Wiley Interscience, 1972); Jean-Paul Fauve and Andre November, *Color and Communication* (Zurich, Switzerland: ABC Editions, 1979); Joseph A. Gatto, *Color and Value: Design Elements* (Worcester, Mass.: Davis Mass, 1974); Konrad Gatz and Wilhelm O. Wallenfang, *Color in Architecture: A Guide to Exterior Design* (New York: Reinhold Publishing Corporation, 1961); Congress of the International Colour Association, *Colour 73, Survey Lectures and Abstracts of the Papers Presented at the Second Congress of the International Colour Association*, The University of York, 2-6 July 1973 (New York: John Wiley and Sons, 1973); Frederick S. Laurence, *Color in Architecture* (New York: National Terra Cotta Society, 1924); William Charles Libby, *Color and the Structural Sense* (Englewood Cliffs, N.J.: Prentice-Hall, Inc., 1974); Donald Pavey, *Color* (Los Angeles: Knapp Press, 1980); Tom Porter and Byron Mikellides, *Color for Architecture* (New York: Van Nostrand Reinhold, 1976); and Patricia Sloane, *Colour: Basic Principles, New Directions* (New York: Reinhold Book Corp, 1967).

The use of color on architectural forms, particularly large public or civic structures both modern and historic has been considered by Martina Duttmann, Friedrich Schmuck, and Johannes Uhl, *Color in Townscape* (San Francisco: W. H. Freeman and Co., 1981); Jonas Gavel, *Colour: A Study of its Position in the Art Theory of the Quattro- and Cinquecento* (Stockholm: Alquist and Wiksell International, 1979); and David Van Zanten, *Architectural Polychromy of the 1830's* (New York: Garland Publishing, Inc., 1977).

As we review these interpretations in the next several sections we will discover that none of them is totally inadequate as an explanation of the patterns of color we observe. But they all fail in some way to cover the range of phenomena we must consider. Together they hint at the possibility of a more satisfying departure for implicitly they suggest how their deficiencies can be overcome. It is a departure which revolves around the idea of communication and it is the development of this idea that is the subject of this dissertation. The study of color, interesting as it is in itself, will serve as the means for testing this departure against its predecessors and competitors, and as a way of questioning our current understanding of the physical aspect of cities, societies, and perhaps entire cultures.

In barest outline this departure will develop the proposition that the built environment, and particularly its coloration, can be viewed as an aspect of material expression in the process of human communication. Communication in this sense will be seen to include verbal and non-verbal behavior as well as the physical objects that most concern us. In effect we will maintain that cultures and societies, in all their manifestations, must be understood from the point of view of the process of communication that connects their components. This departure calls for a reconstitution of our customary idea of communication so as to include more than verbal language (or perhaps non-verbal behavior) in its domain. In another sense this departure calls for the reappraisal of the evidence we use to make inferences about the operation of social forces since it will maintain that these forces are filtered through the communication process. Above all it seeks to anchor our understanding of the properties of human action in the objective features of the physical city.

The Legacy of Interpretations: Questions of Meaning and Mechanism

It is important to see the idea of communication as a logical consequence of rather than as an arbitrary replacement for previous research and theory. This point can be established by reviewing previous interpretive schemes. Such a review can also establish what it means to speak of the physical city as part of the process of human communication, and can indicate how we are both helped and hindered by the literatures, concepts, and methods to which this inquiry is heir.

In examining this legacy we soon discover that no two scholars agree on exactly the messages conveyed between people or upon the mechanisms of their transmission. Moreover some researchers study single channels of communication, as between architect and client, while others look at many channels of transmission from the point of view of a single type of message, say the communication of power or control. As a result, the literature which falls within this project's purview is at once focused and diffuse: focused, because many researchers have concentrated on the mechanics and dynamics of particular systems of material-environmental communication, but diffuse, because the topic of communication and the analytical equipment brought to bear upon it by various scholars have proven to be incompatible. We are left with focused accounts of isolated and sometimes internally consistent systems of meaning but without an organizing principle which might bridge these separate inquiries.

This problem is compounded by the fact that some scholars are more concerned with the content of cultural communication than with its form, just as others demonstrate the obverse inclination and concentrate on analyzing the mechanisms, the logic and the rules of communication, rather than its content. As a consequence the literatures pertinent to this project fall into two, still rather heterogeneous, categories. One contains the work of art and architectural historians and critics, cultural and social geographers, anthropologists, political scientists, sociologists and the like who are interested in the content of messages conveyed through the medium of the constructed landscape. A second body of literature is made up of research by both scholars in many of the same fields and by linguists and semioticians who are interested in the mechanisms of transmission. Associated with this latter corpus, because these mechanisms rely on the human propensity for symbolization, is another large but varied literature concerned with the processes of human symbolization, including semiotics.

General criticisms must be leveled against both categories of literature. In considering research concerned with the content of artifactual communication, it is evident that little effort has been made to realize the full range of inferences about human activity that are derivable from the concept of communication. Even when cultural geographers or students of the landscape choose to view the creation of landscape as a process of communication, they generally fail to follow through and delve into the issues that immediatedly suggest themselves: namely the parallels and differences between the study of the artifactual medium of communication and studies of other modes such as verbal language, typically based on the dubious assumption that meaning is relational, univocal, and independent of context. Many of the insights that can be extracted from previous

studies of language, paralanguage and social behavior as
communication (such as that undertaken in symbolic interactionism)
are for the most part ignored, or remain unincorporated into the
author's methods of analysis. If these ideas are used, the
assumptions behind them are left unquestioned. The analyses often
employ Saussurian, Peircian, or Chomskian terms without a thorough
examination of the validity of these theorist's views of language.
So, once these scholars have alluded to landscape as a medium of
communication they retreat from the implications inherent in the
concept. By interpreting specific systems or fields of meaning they
achieve a limited insight but fail to sustain the vitality and
heuristic appeal of their original assertions.

   The criticism of the second category of literature is keyed
less to omission than to oversight. It has been too easy for
scholars to become overly concerned with the competing claims of
Saussure, Peirce, Morris, Barthes, Langer, Cassirer, Jakobson,
Sapir, Whorf, and others so as to lose sight of the social
importance, variety and content of the messages studied as well as
of the assumptions on which they are based. A priori philosophizing
and reductionist thinking have led to the postulation of direct
analogies between material artifacts and language such that the
landscape might almost be said to speak in sentences and
paragraphs.[2] Not only does this approach emphasize one function of
communication over all others, but it fails to provide a
comprehensive account of human communication. Stressing the
referential and aesthetic functions of transmissions makes it easy
to forget that language, and perhaps communication through
landscape, display social roles, norms, goals, and tasks in a
variety of social contexts where the nuances of intonation, elision,
and usage modify formal structural meaning.

   It is necessary to question the epistemological and
ontological assumptions inherent in these studies. Grammar, sign,
and symbol are theoretical constructs, not a priori features of
reality. To assume that they are the latter is to accept what has
been termed the "Conduit Metaphor"[3] of language. This complex
metaphor seems to provide the foundation for much linguistic
theorizing. Unfortunately its structuring from the assertions that
(1) ideas or meanings are objects, (2) linguistic expressions are

---

2. This extreme form of explanation has been used by Umberto Eco, "A
Componential Analysis of the Architectural Sign /Column/," in *Signs, Symbols, and
Architecture*, eds. Geoffrey Broadbent, Richard Bunt, and Charles Jencks (New
York: John Wiley, 1980), pp. 213-232, and by Gabriela Ghioca, "A Comparative
Analysis of Architectural Signs (Applied to Columns)," *Semiotica* 14 (1975):40-51.

3. Michael J. Reddy, "The Conduit Metaphor," in *Metaphor and Thought,* ed.
Andrew Ortony (Cambridge: Cambridge University Press, 1979), pp. 284-324.

containers and, (3) communication is sending, requires that we regard words, sentences, signs, and symbols as having meaning in themselves, independent of context or user. We must not let this persuasive metaphor and its attendant theoretical constructs cloud our view of communication, a phenomenon of individual and collective human behavior which occurs at many levels and in many highly related modes dependent on context.

The implication of these two general criticisms is that the issues of content, form, and use of material artifacts in human communication must be re-examined. It is necessary to search for commonalities in a discussion which has evolved into a rather disjunct hermeneutic of the content of material communication. Perhaps we can begin the discussion by posing the question of meaning, color, and physical form: what information is conveyed through the use of color, and how can we appraise it? Even if we find that we must subsequently question the usefulness of this formulation, its currency in contemporary discussions justifies its adoption at least rhetorically as an organizing principle.

Perceptual Considerations

We can begin by considering human color perception itself. How essential is a knowledge of human visual capacity to an understanding of color use in the cityscape? We know, for example, that sighted people, save for those afflicted with forms of color blindness, can distinguish millions of colors. Can a description of the neural basis of this fact account for the patterns of color that emerge in cityscapes? If such a description helps us, it is only because the physiological basis for the human response to color can be taken as a set of facts, knowing as we do that it is related to the similarity and contrasts among stimuli, their proximity, continuity, closure, and so forth, just as we are aware that people become accustomed to homogeneous stimulation but readily perceive any contrast with it. These facts are presumably related to an understanding of why vivid colors are used to mark objects in the environment which represent types of danger. Vivid reds and yellows occur infrequently in nature so that when they are used the contrast between their brightness and a generally monochromatic background will be noticed. Their use directs attention to the red-painted stop sign or hazard marker. People or organizations wishing to draw attention to themselves and their own special identity in the cityscape can use color in the same way. Depending on the background, contrast need not always be achieved by the use of vivid hues. On a trip down the Las Vegas "Strip" at night the buildings which are not lit in vivid colors stand out almost as much as those that are.

The facts of perception offer a variety of options for color use, but no justification for their application. They explain how color is patterned to take advantage of the visual organs, but not why people choose to avail themselves of these options in certain situations. Knowledge of visual perception alone provides no explanation for why certain people or groups will choose to mark some hazards and not others, or why they will use color to set themselves apart from their neighbors in some contexts and not in others. We know that social forms can be communicated visually, but an understanding of the perceptual system does not explain why people choose to mark such forms in the first place.

Psychological Considerations

While it is reasonable to downplay the importance of color perception in explanations of color use, we should note that perception theory has on occasion been tied to other theories, particularly those based upon the assumption of an intrinsic psychological symbolism of color. In this case human perception of color is presented as more than a physiological mechanism. At its foundation rests a series of natural psychological templates which guide our manipulation and interpretation of color. For example, vivid red calls attention to itself not necessarily because of contrast with its background, but because it fits a psychological template which associates red with blood and fire. As the expression of an archetype the use of red to mark environmental hazards represents an iconic relation between logical symbolic complements. This interpretive position on color symbolism argues that there is a connection between color use and the associations which stem from our psychological experiences. Insofar as conventions of color use are learned through time the argument has some validity. However, to maintain that there is a natural and intrinsic iconography universally applicable to the interpretation of color use stretches the argument beyond its capacity.

We cannot deny that some patterns of color use do seem to relate to psychological archetypes or prototypes. This is true in particular with respect to ritual and formal ceremonial occasions where a natural color symbolism does suggest itself. Key religious observances as well as important events in the history of political states are framed in colors associated with distinct meanings: white with purity or innocence; green with rebirth and regeneration; black with death and mourning; red with the emotions of both love and hate; violet with love and truth, or passion and suffering, and so forth.[4] However, most patterns of color use are

8

far more heterogenous and much less consistent than these. They juxtapose colors in ways which cannot be made logically compatible with any single system of color symbolism.

In our culture red can be associated with crime or sin (red-light districts), love (St. Valentine's Day imagery), hate ("seeing everything in red"), the movement of traffic (red lights and stop signs), the season of Pentecost among Christians, political beliefs (reds and rednecks), ethnicity (red-skinned), profitability (red ink), warnings of impending conflict or danger (red alert), and with many other items. It is difficult to argue that red houses, fire stations, red-light districts, red barns, and stop signs all share some characteristic which justifies their use of red. This is not to deny that in any particular context it will be possible to establish the significance of red to human action. This meaning may in some instances be related to archetypical forms. However there are few situations where color can be assessed on the basis of an encompassing and consistent set of such archetypes.

In applying symbolic interpretation scholars have striven for consistency beyond the conditions of everyday life. People respond to color in many different ways depending on how and when it is used. Thus it would generally be a mistake, or at least unenlightening, to explain the use of color on a suburban house on the basis of the symbolic protocols of religious or psychological experience. On a city street already painted in vivid colors someone might paint a house bright red only because it sets that building off from its neighbors, not because red is more meaningful than any other hue.

Nevertheless, no matter how we downplay the role of perception or the deterministic application of psychological principles to the study of color use, we can not afford to overlook them completely. There may, in fact, be psychological or physiological imperatives which are important to understanding the social use of color. They may oblige us sometimes to recast explanations of the kind put forth by this project's conception of communication. Let us say, for example, that we believe preferences for foods are an accurate sign of social class. Although people of a particular culture all have the same foods available to them, people of one class often prefer only one kind of food while those of a second class may prefer another. Is this a case where food preference frames class affiliation? If we discover that the first class of people suffer from a genetic disorder which induces an allergic reaction whenever

---

4. George Ferguson, *Signs and Symbols in Christian Art* (New York: Oxford University Press, 1981), pp. 151-152.

they partake of food outside their normal dietary range, we can
hardly maintain that preference for food is an indicator of
voluntary patterns of class affiliation. It defines only those who
suffer from this genetic malady. Dietary customs could still be
treated as part of human communication but their significance to the
process would change.

Matters of culture, in general, are related in part to
questions of genetics, physiology, or psychology. Might it be
possible to refer some socially significant patterns of color use
basically to these imperatives? Although such a relegation may be
possible now with respect to some phenomena, it is hardly plausible
for the subject of the present study. The patterns of color we
experience in our own culture, as well as a multitude of
cross-cultural observations, militate against psychological or
physiological explanations of their origin or present prevalence.

Surely this is a peremptory and in some ways a premature
statement. There is at some point a limit to the applicability of
the type of analysis this project advocates. However, it must be
understood that the social patterns to which the project is
addressed are impressed on the structure of society. The rapidity
with which color patterns can change within societies and across
cultures to mark short-lived fashions and conventions of social
interaction distances them from the slowly changing barriers which
ultimately are under study in the present context.

The Varieties of Meaning

Observation of the many meanings elicited by a single color
make it easy to discredit any explanation which might link patterns
of urban color use to an intrinsic, unitary color symbolism.
Nevertheless, some scholars have advanced the proposition that,
although color may not be assigned a unitary meaning, there are
regularities to its use. Color attains meaning, or "functions," at
a variety of levels no two of which assign it the same meaning, but
when taken together encompass all possibilities.

This idea has been used to draw a parallel between the
"meanings" of color (or physical attributes generally) and the
functions of language. Just as each function implies a different
meaning for a word, many meanings revolve around a single use of
color. In the realm of architectural forms, Preziosi has attempted
to catalogue functions and associated meanings.[5] His designations of

---

5. Donald Preziosi, *The Semiotics of the Built Environment: An
Introduction to Architectonic Analysis* (Bloomington: Indiana University Press,
1979), pp. 61-73, and also in his *Architecture, Language, and Meaning* (The Hague:
Mouton Publishers, 1979), pp. 47-57. Indirectly Preziosi's account of the
functions of language are related to Jakobson's discussion of the same in

function have been adopted for the discussion that follows, which develops their bearing on the interpretation of color phenomena. The same categories might be applied to the literature concerned with the meaning or function of physical forms in general. Even though a review of this literature, thus organized, might be of interest to some readers, at this point it would unduly hamper the discussion. Citations from the literature are presented in a supplementary bibliography at the end of this monograph.

The Referential Function

Perhaps most attention has been given to the ways in which physical artifacts "symbolize" or specify their usage. Typically the questions is seen as one of reference or of the semantics by which types of social forms signal their immediate purposes through material and architectonic forms. This occurs in every subsystem of society, and concerns individuals as well as the largest collectivities. Subsystemic functions of adaptation, goal attainment, integration, and pattern maintenance are registered in the symbolism of economic, political, social, and cultural function.

Many of the patterns of color use found in the city appear to serve a referential function. Banks, restaurants, and shops tend each to use different color schemes to frame their functional role. Further, colors are used to mark small differences among organizations which share the same general function. Groups offering less expensive goods and services than their competitors as a rule use more colors and in particular more vivid colors. Those which seek to offer similar goods or services to even slightly different clienteles sometimes also use distinguishing ranges of colors. Thus women's clothing stores are generally colored differently from men's clothing shops.

The Aesthetic Function

Often the aesthetic level is seen as the only level at which color attains meaning. In this view, color serves only to help make a building or a city visually pleasing (or in common parlance "beautiful"). The pursuit of this idea stands behind just about all discussions of color use in relation to the architectural design process. Books on the subject do point out that color should be used to mark clearly the function of a structure (its referential function), and perhaps the activity patterns that are to be enclosed (the territorial and exhortative functions yet to be introduced), but the conception of a natural color harmony or aesthetic is dominant.

"Linguistics and Poetics," in *Style in Language,* ed. Thomas Sebeok (Bloomington: Indiana University Press, 1960), pp. 350-377.

Although it is clear that color use can sustain assessments based upon aesthetic function, it is necessary to stress that such assessments are among the least satisfying of explanations. This is especially true where it is maintained that aesthetic values depend upon absolute and fixed principles of perception. It is far more productive to proceed from the premise that aesthetic judgments are relative to the people who make them and to the period in which they are made. In a sense aesthetic interpretations reveal more about the people and period that shape them than about the physical properties of color itself.6

The Allusory, Connotative, or Meta-Architectonic Function

With regard to color this function is compatible with natural systems of symbolism. It proposes that there are symbolic archetypes which in our culture, for example, associate the use of red on stop signs with blood. These allusory uses of color are often designed to attract attention and are sometimes very compelling. Chicago's fire academy displays a great deal of red tile, presumably by way of alluding to fire while gold filigree on church alters and spires is seen by some people as alluding to the riches of heaven.

The Phatic-Territorial Function

Some of our most direct if little-noticed experiences with color involve the phatic-territorial function.7 On city streets each building or organizational facade tends to be set apart from its neighbors by a more or less distinct color scheme. The end of one design and a change to some other pattern may mark the limits of an organization's territory or indicate the boundaries of group sociability. Construction sites and playing fields are often surrounded by uniformly colored borders. All in all, color serves as a frequent marker of the territory or boundaries of many types of social action.

---

6. Aesthetic distinctions are often interesting only insofar as their exercise and popularization serve to mark social class or affiliation. Thus, just as patterns of intonation, articulation, grammar, and vocabulary serve to distinguish social groups, the ability to make aesthetic distinctions of specific types concerning the use of color may serve a similar function.

7. Phatic refers to the act of employing speech for the purpose of revealing and sharing feelings or establishing an atmosphere of sociability rather than for communicating ideas. Here its meaning is taken in a broader sense so as to include non-verbal behavior and the use of material artifacts, as well as speech, when they are used to define an interactional domain of contact between people.

*The Emotive or Expressive
Function*

For many people the emotive effects of color are of the highest importance. People often express their mood in the colors they choose to wear, in the colors of their homes, or in the colors of their cars. Their choices may rest upon the facts of human visual perception, and probably can be traced in part to the allusory meanings of color use that are acquired with experience. It seems reasonable to maintain that people take advantage of these facts and conventions to signal their emotional valence with regard to particular activities through color in costume, and in interior and exterior design.

The Exhortative Function

In this function, color gives commands. The traffic signal is perhaps the best example of the employment of color in this capacity, but there are many other instances of color coding which demand that their appearance be followed by an appropriate action.

The Semiotic Model

The preceding functions may not seem to be logical complements, but from the point of view of semiotic models they can be shown to be compatible at a higher level of abstraction. Although difficult to characterize in total, most applications of semiotic theory rely upon a view of society as an elaborate system of signs and symbols.[8] All human action including physical artifacts, colors, words, and so forth can be seen as playing a part in this system. Accordingly, actions and objects are rarely meaningful in isolation; they must be assessed in relation to the way they stand in for other actions and objects, as regularized by an elaborate network of codes and conventions which specify the connotative and denotative meaning of these forms.

Some forms are called symbols because of the arbitrariness of their linkage with their objects. Some are called icons because of a resemblance to their objects. Some are called indices because they are physically contiguous with their objects. As a field rising above all of these distinctions, semiotics has been defined

---

8. The problem of characterizing the term "semiotics" is the primary reason it was not used in the title of this monograph. To label this work "A Semiotic of the Urban Built Environment" (and to regard it as part of a more general investigation of the semiotics of material form), is to invite misinterpretation. Although this writer would be willing to adopt the term as proposed by Margaret Mead as "patterned communications in all modalities" (T.A. Sebeok, A.S. Hayes, and M.C. Bateson, eds., *Approaches to Semiotics* [The Hague: Mouton, 1964], p. 5), it is not possible for him to subscribe to a now prevalent definition of semiotics as the scientific study of signs and symbols. Acceptance of the latter definition forces one to accept, implicitly, certain theoretical assumptions which, in fact, would seem to prevent sustained scientific inquiry by means of the semiotic model. These assumptions and their effect on theorizing are the subject, for the most part, of the remainder of this chapter.

as the scientific study of signs, or of the symbolic content of
social form. As it pertains to physical expression, many authors
have contributed to or criticized this emerging discipline.9

The functions specified above when regarded from the semiotic
viewpoint, take on the semblance of levels of meaning rather than
criteria in conflict. The use of color in one way need not rule out
its use in another. Scholars do often specialize in assessing the
functional meaning of color (or of the physical attributes),
selecting only one or two of these levels. This practice simply
represents the division of scarce labor in the face of a large and
complex task. Their efforts need not be regarded as contradictory.

Problems with the Semiotic Model

Regardless of its advantages, the semiotic model is still
faced with problems that are not easily resolved. It is unclear how
the functional categories of meaning relate to an individual's
appraisal of the full range of physical objects or color patterns.
People do not interpret material artifacts of communication with
reference to only one or two of these functions and any person's
reading of these forms may be very different from that of others at
just about any level. It is difficult to believe that apartments,
highways, and cathedrals convey the same sorts of information to

---

9. A survey of the recent literature of semiotics might include Roland
Barthes, *Elements of Semiology* (New York: Hill and Wang, 1967); Jean
Baudrillard, *Le Systeme des Objets* (Paris: Gallimard, 1968) and *Pour une Critique
de l'Economie Politique du Signe* (Paris: Gallimard, 1972); Seymour Chatman,
Umberto Eco, and Jean-Marie Klinkenberg, eds., *A Semiotic Landscape,* Proceedings
of the First Congress of the International Association for Semiotic Studies,
Milan, June 1974, (The Hague: Mouton Publishers, 1979); Rosalind Coward and John
Ellis, *Language and Materialism: Developments in Semiology and the Theory of the
Subject* (London: Routledge and Kegan Paul, 1977); Janet L. Dolgin, David S.
Kemnitzer, and David M. Schneider, eds., *Symbolic Anthropology: A Reader in the
Study of Symbols and Meanings* (New York: Columbia University Press, 1977);
Umberto Eco, *A Theory of Semiotics* (Bloomington: Indiana University Press,
1976); Pierre Guiraud, *Semiology* (London: Routledge and Kegan Paul, 1975);
Terence Hawkes, *Structuralism and Semiotics* (Berkeley: University of California
Press, 1977); Gyorgy Kepes, ed., *Sign, Image, Symbol* (New York: George
Braziller, 1966); Martin Krampen, *Meaning in the Urban Environment* (London: Pion
Ltd., 1979); Ladislav Matejka and Irwin R. Titunik, eds., *Semiotics of Art:
Prague School Contributions* (Cambridge, MA; MIT Press, 1976); Jan Mukarovsky,
Structure, Sign, and Function: Selected Essays by Jan Mukarovsky (New Haven,
Conn.: Yale University Press, 1978); Luis J. Prieto, *Messages et Signaux* (Paris:
Presses Universitaires de France, 1966); David M. Rasmussen, *Symbol and
Interpretation* (The Hague: Martinus Hijhoff, 1974); Jurgen Ruesch, ed., *Semiotic
Approaches to Human Relations* (The Hague: Mouton, 1972); Thomas A. Sebeok, ed., *A
Perfusion of Signs* (Bloomington: Indiana University Press, 1977); Thomas A.
Sebeok, A.S. Hayes, and M.C. Bateson, eds., *Approaches to Semiotics* (The Hague:
Mouton, 1964); Milton Singer, "For a Semiotic Anthropology," in *Sight, Sound,
and Sense,* ed. Thomas A. Sebeok (Bloomington: Indiana University Press, 1978),
pp. 202-231 and "Signs of the Self: An Exploration in Semiotic Anthropology,"
American Anthropologist 82 (September 1980):485-507; and Mieczyslaw Wallis, *Arts
and Signs* (Indiana University Publications, Studies in Semiotics, vol. 2.
Bloomington: Indiana University Publications, Studies in Semiotics, 1975) and
"Semantic and Symbolic Elements in Architecture: Iconology as a First Step
Towards an Architectural Semiotic," *Semiotica* 8 (1973):220-238.

Some criticisms of the semiotic outlook are provided by Manfredo Tafuri,
Architecture and Utopia: Design and Capitalist Development (Cambridge: MIT
Press, 1976), pp.150-169, and *Theories and History of Architecture* (New York:
Harper & Row, Publishers, 1980), pp. 103-139, as well as by Roger Scruton, *The
Aesthetics of Architecture* (Princeton, N.J.: Princeton University Press, 1979),
pp. 158-178, and Dan Sperber, *Rethinking Symbolism* (Cambridge: Cambridge
University Press, 1975).

each member of their viewing public. Yet published research in semiotics suggests that they do, and that the messages conveyed by different forms are so distinct and emphatic as to obviate the the relevance of the levels that have been discussed. Each form is seen as implying the use of a separate type of symbol. This kind of analysis fails to recognize that these artifacts can figure in communicative interactions at many of the same levels (i.e. all can be interpreted aesthetically, they are all capable of emotive expression, and each can refer and connote). The extent to which they do so may be a question of degree and context. Their relegation to symbolic categories prevents their incorporation into a more encompassing theory of human communication.

Of course most people typically do not spend the same effort looking for an aesthetic message in the ordinary structures of the landscape that they would when contemplating a cathedral. Conversely, people will be less concerned with the referential markers which assure efficient pedestrian flow through cathedrals than with traffic signs on a busy street. It is the rare analysis which looks for the arcane and allusory symbolism thought to be appropriate to cathedrals in the form of highways and shopping centers.[10] The subtle messages concerning social territories and people's sense of place apparent in an apartment complex are not often searched for in a cathedral. The so-called message has become the master of our concept of communicational processes and we fail to see symbols as but a theoretical categorization of human communication.

That highways are not repositories of elaborate systems of aesthetic symbolism does not mean that their users do not appreciate them aesthetically at the very instant they are used as iconic markers or social barriers, or that the territories these roads come to delimit are any less important for communication than the referential function of transportation they are designed for. Likewise the religiously symbolic and aesthetic aspects of a cathedral do not mean that the building itself cannot serve as a territorial marker, as an emotive sign, or as a key to understanding continued social and personal bonding among members of its congregation.

The desire of many researchers to dwell on a single line of analysis, to pursue one methodological departure, or to seek out one

---

10. Nevertheless such iconographic studies have been undertaken by Robert Venturi, Denise Scott Brown, and Steven Izenour, *Learning from Las Vegas: The Forgotten Symbolism of Architectural Form* (Cambridge: MIT Press, 1972), and J.B. Jackson, *The Necessity for Ruins, and other Topics* (Amherst: University of Massachusetts Press, 1980).

type of meaning has seriously hampered scholarly recognition of the array of meanings that can be assigned to an object. Not only can a cathedral convey aesthetic, emotive, referential, territorial and allusory meaning, messages, and information through its use in particular contexts, but messages keyed to these dimensions can be in most cases registered by a viewer or user simultaneously. Their separate description and analysis is only a convenience; it would be difficult to describe or analyze the meaning of landscapes if all "readings" had to be described at once. Nevertheless, it is easy to see that it would be helpful to have some analytical model which conceded the polysemic nature of material communication. This model would allow us at least to specify the ways in which material forms are capable of assuming meaning even if individual forms in the landscape capture our attention along only one or two of the possible axes of significance. At present we must be satisfied to capture the dynamism of the normal communicational process in a series of synchronic, uniplanar, or unidimensional snapshots.

Another difficulty: it is unclear how the list of functions derived from the semiotic model can explain synonymous and homonymous forms. How can we account for, first, physical objects which vary in form but have the same meaning and, second, objects which have exactly the same form but are assigned different meanings? In terms of color use, if the traffic lights at an intersection are out, people will still come to a stop if a police officer is providing hand signals. The police officer's gestures and the colored traffic lights are synonymous with respect to the movement of traffic. On the other hand people will not react to a red light on a furnace as they would to a traffic light. Its appearance on the furnace only indicates that the burner or pilot flame is lit. The red lights are homonymous forms.

The problem of reconciling homonymous and synonymous forms to the semiotic model is similar to the one we faced earlier in trying to accommodate the many uses of red within a single system of color symbolism. In that case it was clear that the variety of meanings red can attain are too diverse to be explained by a single interpretive principle. Now we see that even by increasing the number of ways color can "mean" something we cannot explain why an individual in one setting will act as though a color means one thing while in another, will react to the same color quite differently. People are not confused by these homonymous and synonymous forms even if our model is. We are now able to see why this problem arises.

The problem lies in the fact that scholars who have attempted explanations based upon the functional cataloguing of meaning have

inadvertantly fixed upon an inappropriate object of study. In the
human use of material forms we observe two features: the objects
themselves, and the contexts within which they are suspended. At
least up to a point the relation of object and context is symbiotic.
Context does define the significance of objects, but an object does
not usually define the entire context within which it is found.
While the mapping of context onto object is in some ways definite an
unique, the relation of object to context is ambiguous. Context
must be defined in relation to human action and the propagation of
this action. It would be a mistake to develop a classificatory
schema of human symbolic action based upon the qualities of objects
alone. A categorization of this type provides us with no way to
incorporate context into our theory.

Nonetheless, it is one or another version of the semiotic
strategy which most scholars of communication have chosen to adopt.
As a consequence they have overlooked the fact that our efforts
should be directed toward understanding the context within which
action takes place and objects are used. The focus of study must be
observable human action and behavior. It is this phenomenon from
which the use of material objects arises and attains significance.
Of course the confusion with regard to a proper orientation of study
is understandable. The material and behavioral manifestations of
interaction are readily discernible, whereas the definition of
context is not; it relates to a complicated genealogy of interaction
extending through time and space. Pursuit of this orientation is
necessary for future research.

The Linguistic Analogy

Most scholars studying landscape and communication have turned
to linguistics and philosophy for a solution to some of their
problems. This is evident from even a cursory survey of the
literature. Broadbent, Jencks, Eco, Agrest, Gandelsonas, and many
others have relied upon these fields, borrowing terms from Saussure,
Peirce, Chomsky, and other major theorists.[11] Although some novel

---

11 . Geoffrey Broadbent, Richard Bunt, and Charles Jencks, eds., *Signs,
Symbols, and Architecture* (New York: John Wiley, 1980); Charles Jencks and
George Baird, eds., *Meaning in Architecture* (New York: George Braziller, 1966);
Umberto Eco, "A Componential Analysis of the Architectural Sign /Column/," in
Signs, Symbols, and Architecture, ed. Geoffrey Broadbent, Richard Bunt, and
Charles Jencks (New York: John Wiley, 1980), pp. 213-232, *A Theory of Semiotics*
(Bloomington: Indiana University Press, 1976), and "Function and Sign: The
Semiotics of Architecture," in *Signs, Symbols, and Architecture,* ed. Geoffrey
Broadbent, Richard Bunt, and Charles Jencks (New York: John Wiley, 1980), pp.
11-79; Diana Agrest and Mario Gandelsonas, "Critical Remarks on Semiology and
Architecture," *Semiotica* 9 (1974):252-271, "Semiotics and Architecture:
Ideological Consumption or Theoretical Work,' *Oppositions* 1 (1973):93-100, and
"Semiotics and the Limits of Architecture," in *A Perfusion of Signs,* ed. Thomas
A. Sebeok (Bloomington: Indiana University Press, 1977), pp. 90-120; Mario
Gandelsonas, "From Structure to Subject: The Formation of an Architectural

formulations have been put forward--some indigenous to anthropology--all but those from ecology and symbolic interactionism share a structural foundation reminiscent of linguistic formulations.[12] These models can be seen as the source of the difficulties of which we are now aware.

Some critics, such as Guillerme, hold that these deficiencies result from a spurious analogy drawn between architecture and language.[13] He would have us believe that the reason so much of the research derived from this analogy proves at least partly inadequate is that linguistic models, while fitting language well enough, do not really model the functions of architecture. This project hopes to show that Guillerme's position is misdirected. It argues that the analogy has been ineffective because of defects in linguistic theory, not because of the inapplicability of the analogy per se. Architectural theorists have borrowed theories of language without sufficiently questioning their assumptions. The language analogy, which might have guided us toward more profitable investigations, has prevented us from realizing that language and architecture are complementary parts of a single general process of human communication. We need a model capable of encompassing this larger process.

We must recognize that inadequacies are not confined solely to the application of linguistic models to artifactual aspects of communication. Various linguistic theorists have come to realize that deficiencies are also to be found in the application of linguistic models to their own object of study, namely language.[14]

Language," *Oppositions* 17 (Summer 1979):6-29; Chris Abel, "The Language Analogy in Architectural Theory and Criticism; Some Remarks in the Light of Wittgenstein's Linguistic Relativism," *Architectural Association Quarterly* 12 (1980):39-47; V. Markuzon, "An Attempt to Redefine the 'Language of Architecture' in Terms of Semantics," *Architectural Association Quarterly* 4 (1972):41-48; Christian Norberg-Schulz, "Kahn, Heidegger and the Language of Architecture," *Oppositions* 18 (Fall 1979):28-47.

12. Some important recent works in the field of symbolic interactionism include Herbert Blumer, *Symbolic Interactionism: Perspective and Method* (Englewood Cliffs, N.J.: Prentice-Hall, 1969); E. Gordon Erickson, *The Territorial Experience: Human Ecology as Symbolic Interaction,* with a Foreword by Herbert Blumer (Austin: University of Texas Press, 1980); Bernard N. Meltzer, John W. Petras, and Larry T. Reynolds. *Symbolic Interactonism: Genesis, Varieties, and Criticism* (London: Routledge and Kegan Paul, 1975); Sheldon Stryker, *Symbolic Interactionism: A Social Structural Version* (Menlo Park, Cal.: Benjamin/Cummings, 1980).

13. Jacques Guillerme, "The Idea of Architectural Language: A Critical Review," *Oppositions* 10 (Fall 1977):21-26.

14. Roy Harris, *The Language Myth* (New York: St. Martin's Press, 1981); George Lakoff and Mark Johnson, *Metaphors We Live By* (Chicago: University of Chicago Press, 1980); I. A. Richards, *The Philosophy of Rhetoric* (New York: Oxford University Press, 1936); and Victor H. Yngve, "The Struggle for a Theory of Native Speaker" in *A Festschrift for Native Speaker,* ed. Florian Coulmas (The Hague: Mouton, 1981), pp. 29-49, "The Dilemma of Contemporary Linguistics," in *The First Lacus Forum, 1974,* eds. Adam Makkai and Valerie Becker Makkai (Columbia, S.C.: Hornbeam Press, 1975), and "Human Linguistics: The Scientific Study of How People Communicate" (Unpublished MS, University of Chicago, Chicago, IL, revised 1980).

Many scholars in an effort to re-found their respective disciplines
have tried to circumvent these difficulties with theoretical
epicycles rather than to admit their irremovability. Using Yngve as
our guide,[15] let us now turn to some of the chief deficiencies of
linguistic theory.

Assumptions of Linguistic, Symbolist, and Semiotic Theory

*The Assumption that Language
and Systems of Symbols are
Uniform or Homogenous*

The concept of language has long been linked to a presumption
of its uniformity and homogeneity. In part this position is tied to
a normative goal, the establishment of standard language, which
implies that the abstraction of an ideal speaker-listener existing
in an homogenous speech community is accurate and useful.

Scientific linguistics has long repudiated the goal of
prescribing usage, yet rejecting the concomitant presumptions of
uniformity and homogeneity has been problematic. Years of
empirical observation and description of living languages, systems
of communication, and hierarchies of "symbols" have documented
extensive spatial, temporal, and social variation. The variation is
ubiquitous, not particular, and it forces a questioning of a
paradigm according to which individual usage is but the
idiosyncratic corruption of uniform patterns within a system of
symbolic usage. Yet theoretical linguistics still holds to this
assumption.

It could be argued that, since an assumption should be
accepted only as a first approximation, its control of theorizing
could be relaxed when our grasp of language and human symbol systems
is more complete. Unfortunately this assumption has not been
treated in this way. It is no longer open to question and
examination and it is not possible to see how its control can ever
be relaxed. It has been encased in theory to the point where
researchers feel little need to even address diversity with anything
but a nod and wave of the hand.

---

15. Victor H. Yngve, "The Struggle for a Theory of Native Speaker" in *A Festschrift for Native Speaker,* ed. Florian Coulmas (The Hague: Mouton, 1981), pp. 29-49; "The Dilemma of Contemporary Linguistics," in *The First Lacus Forum, 1974,* eds. Adam Makkai and Valerie Becker Makkai (Columbia, S.C.: Hornbeam Press, 1975), "Human Linguistics: The Scientific Study of How People Communicate" (Unpublished MS, University of Chicago, Chicago, IL, revised 1980); and "On the Assumptions of Linguistics," (Unpublished paper, University of Chicago, Department of Linguistics, Chicago, IL, revised December 1981).

The Assumption that Language
and Symbols are Independent
of Situational Context

Traditional linguistic or communicational theory presumes that language and the use of symbols are independent of situational context, that users of language or "symbols" will know what to say in any given situation but that language itself is independent of these situations. In part this assumption derives from a historical accident. Language was long seen as part of the theory of knowledge and, since the focus of this theory was the discovery of immutable truths, truth being independent of context, the study of language as an understanding of statements of truth assumed independence also. The independence of grammar, sign, and symbol became imbedded in the tradition.

However, today we recognize language and the use of "symbols" is very much context dependent. Ambiguous and homonymic forms are rarely a problem in actual use. People recognize their meaning from context. Yet observation as to how expressions are conditioned by, depend on, or are related to the circumstances of their use has not been undertaken widely. Such observations can only lead to dissonance confusion when framed by the traditional assumption of context independence.

The Assumption that Language
and Symbols are Created by
a Point of View

It has always been difficult to find satisfactory definitions for critical linguistic and symbolist terms: language, meaning, grammar, word, sign, icon, symbol and so forth. As Saussure has pointed out

> other sciences work with objects that are given in advance and that can be considered from different viewpoints, but not linguistics...far from it being the object that antedates the viewpoint, it would seem that it is the viewpoint that creates the object...16

Traditional linguistic and symbolist research has tended to confuse its theoretical constructs with the phenomena which it seeks to model. Thus, the concepts of language, grammar, word, and symbol are seen as somehow grounded in the psychological reality of their users. This is not the case. These concepts are theoretical abstractions of particular aspects of the human communicative experience. The fact that they are not bounded by objective criteria in the domain of human action and physical reality reflects badly on the tradition.

---

16. Ferdinand de Saussure, *Course in General Linguistics* (New York: McGraw-Hill Co., 1959), p. 8.

*The Assumption that Language
and Symbolism are Relations
Between Sound (or Object)
and Meaning*

Under this assumption, linguistics is a study of the direct relation between sound (or object) and meaning. The concepts of signifier (sound or object) and signified (meaning) derive from the Stoic dialectic theory of the sign, but there are several difficulties with various facets of the tradition that has passed these concepts on to us. First, modern linguistics and semiotics are little concerned with the theory of knowledge which gave rise to the Stoic theory (the search for truth and a predisposition to conceive of language as propositional). Second, the theory of the sign transmitted in the tradition has been regarded not as an hypothesis but as a foundational assumption. We can quote from several influential linguists:

> The linguistic sign unites, not a thing and a name, but a concept and a sound-image. The latter is not the material sound, a purely physical thing, but the psychological imprint of the sound, the impression that it makes on our senses. The sound-image is sensory, and if I happen to call it "material," it is only in that sense, and by way of opposing it to the other term of the association, the concept, which is generally more abstract...17

> To put it briefly, in human speech, different sounds have different meanings. To study this coordination of certain sounds with certain meanings is to study language.18

> A language, by its nature, relates sounds (or graphs, i.e. marks on paper or the like) to meanings...19

> A grammar of a language, in the sense in which I will use this term, can be loosely described as a system of rules that expresses the correspondence between sound and meaning in this language.20

> Language is a system which mediates, in a highly complex way, between the universe of meaning and the universe of sound.21

> For the speaker and listener speech sounds necessarily act as carriers of meaning. Sound and meaning are, both for language and for linguistics, an indissoluble duality.22

The concept of the sign in statements such as these does carry an implication of discreteness. In this respect perhaps the theory is justified, but it would be better if we could examine that issue separately rather than have it introduced as a basic assumption.

The position adopted by Saussure and many modern linguists,

---

17. Ferdinand de Saussure, *Course in General Linguistics* (New York: McGraw-Hill Co., 1959), p. 8.

18. Leonard Bloomfield, *Language* (New York: Henry Holt and Co., 1933), p. 27.

19. Sydney M. Lamb, *Outline of Stratificational Grammar* (Washington, D.C.: Georgetown University Press, 1966), p. 1.

20. Noam Chomsky, "Deep Structure, Surface Structure, and Semantic Interpretation," in *Studies in General and Oriental Linguistics,* Presented to Shiro Hattori on the Occasion of his Sixtieth Birthday, eds. Roman Jakobson and Shigeo Kanamoto (Tokyo: TEC Co., 1970), p. 52.

21. Wallace L. Chafe, *Meaning and the Structure of Language* (Chicago: University of Chicago Press, 1970), p. 15.

22. Roman Jakobson, *The Framework of Language,* Michigan Studies in the Humanities, no. 1 (Ann Arbor: University of Michigan, Horace H. Rackham School of Graduate Studies, 1980), p. 95.

logicians, and philosophers, focuses unwarranted attention on the standard case of a one-to-one relation between sound and meaning unified in the sign. Lack of one-to-one correspondence is necessarily considered an anomaly in the associated theory of knowledge, for it is important to have clear and unambiguous statements in logical arguments about what is true and false. We have known for a long time that if language is a relation, it must be much more complex than a simple sign relation, yet the supposed correspondence of sounds and meanings is all too frequently assumed as given, or invoked loosely by those who know better. Piaget, for example, says:

> Every word in a language designates a concept, which constitutes its signification.[23]

One page of a dictionary, or a moment spent in contemplating words such as "of," "the," "run," or words from other languages such as the French "faire," should be sufficient to remind us that such statements cannot be true of language.

The Assumption that Language or Symbols Express Meaning

This assumption is best stated by Chomsky:

> Let us assume, given two universal language-independent systems of representation, a phonetic system for the specification of sound and a semantic system for the specification of meaning. As to the former, there are many concrete proposals... In the domain of semantics there are, needless to say, problems of fact and principle that have barely been approached, and there is no reasonably concrete or well-defined "theory of semantic representation" to which one can refer. I will however, assume here that such a system can be developed, and that it makes sense to speak of the ways in which the inherent meaning of a sentence, characterized in some still-to-be-discovered system of representation, is related to various aspects of its form.[24]

After more than two thousand years language is still supposed to relate sound to meaning, but problems with the concept of meaning "have barely been approached." It remains far from clear just what meaning is supposed to be, after much effort over the centuries has been spent in trying to discover its true nature.[25] A generation of linguists tried to get around the problem by explicitly not dealing with meaning. It was hoped that work starting at the sound or object end of the relation would eventually push far enough to allow meaning to be treated in a rigorous way. Recent work in semantics has served to bring back many of the old problems, but few have questioned the necessity of a concept of meaning. Meaning has never

---

23. Jean Piaget, *Structuralism* (New York: Harper and Row, 1970), p. 74.

24. Noam Chomsky, "Deep Structure, Surface Structure, and Semantic Interpretation," in *Studies in General and Oriental Linguistics,* Presented to Shiro Hattori on the Occasion of his Sixtieth Birthday, eds. Roman Jakobson and Shigeo Kanamoto (Tokyo: TEC Co., 1970), p. 52.

25. A classic statement belongs to C. K. Ogden and I. A. Richards, *The Meaning of Meaning: A Study of the Influence of Language upon Thought and of the Science of Symbolism* (New York: Harcourt, Brace, and World, Inc., 1923).

been observed as solid data or measured and recorded in the way that sound has, yet theories continue to be based on a belief in its existence. Even if our popular speech takes meaning to be a substance and would have it carried or conveyed by symbol or sound from speaker to hearer, like so much freight on a train, it must be very insubstantial.

It is probably no accident that we have inherited these assumptions. Reddy[26] and, later, Lakoff and Johnson[27] make the point that linguistic theorizing has been captured, quite unintentionally, by what might be termed the Conduit Metaphor. It is. built up from these analogies: that words are like containers for thoughts, that communication is like the channeling of containers to others, and the comprehension is like the unpacking of these conceptual objects. This metaphor is deeply rooted in our culture. Even our casual references to communication and language make use of it.[28] Unfortunately, the ease with which it allows us to view language as uniform, propositional, and context-free, as if unambiguous circuits linked signifier, significant, and signified on a one-to-one basis, prevents us from seeing language as the complicated negotiation that it more closely resembles. Each transaction requires that a context of mutuality be established and a domain of control be defined before the referring anaphoric functions of language can be realized. Perhaps a guiding metaphor of language-as-transaction (or interaction) would be more appropriate for language and material semiosis.

Summary

When considering the human use of color or of physical objects and their attributes in general we cannot ignore the heuristic appeal of the idea of symbol. The value of the concept lies in the way it directs our attention away from the features of an object's immediate use and toward an understanding of its place in a web of social action and meaning. Objects and actions cannot always be taken at face value; they often stand in for or symbolize other actions or interactions. Social action cannot always be interpreted at one level.

---

26 . Michael J. Reddy, "The Conduit Metaphor," in *Metaphor and Thought*, ed. Andrew Ortony (Cambridge: Cambridge University Press, 1979), pp. 284-324.

27 . George Lakoff and Mark Johnson, *Metaphors We Live By* (Chicago: University of Chicago Press, 1980).

28 . Reddy gives one hundred forty-one distinct expressions or expressive paradigms which all refer to verbal communication in a manner consonant with the Conduit Metaphor in "The Conduit Metaphor," in Ortony, pp. 311-320.

In some ways it is useful to see color as language. Our attention is then drawn to nuances of form which somehow parallel the subtleties of linguistic or textual interpretation. We can begin, for example, to see the analysis of color in the cityscape as a study in iconology. The concepts of metaphor, metonymy, homonymy, simile can sometimes even approach the status of explanations. These ideas lead to a further appreciation of the many levels at which color can be read.

Nonetheless, when traditional linguistic theory has been confronted by the polysemic, context-dependent features of human communication the result has not been especially insightful. Attempts to incorporate the concepts of homonymous usage and context have given rise to involved doctrinal addenda which have pulled theory further and further away from direct explanation of generalized communicative phenomena.

It is true that linguistic concepts have led to valuable multidisciplinary excursions into the various realms of symbol use. Yet too often researchers have tried to establish unique meanings for the signs and symbols of human interaction without first defining the dimensions of their context. They are surprised when scholars from other disciplines perceive their work as incorrect or incomplete. A litany of exegesis and critical refrain occurs so frequently that it obscures our recognition of the fact that all of the attempted interpretations may be correct, depending, of course, on context. While disciplinary discussions have gone far in illuminating the cultural use of symbols, they have at the same time drawn attention away from a questioning of the assumptions lying behind any search for meaning or significance. Too often researchers have tried to formulate their goals as the search for "a" meaning of signs and symbols evident in human interaction, as a sort of mapping of meaning on to symbol. As a result, our inventory or catalogue of meaning has grown continually.

In the end we are fortunate to have available a rich literature based upon observations of human symbolic action, and going far to underpin this project's conceptual foundation. The fact that this literature presents distinct theoretical problems is not an insurmountable obstacle as we will see in the next chapter.

CHAPTER II

A COMMUNICATIONS APPROACH TO THE STUDY OF SOCIAL ACTION

A General Outline

The interpretations introduced in chapter I, taken together, suggest that color, and more generally physical objects with all of their attributes, are related to flows of information. The person or group that uses color is somehow providing information to other people, and all are engaged in communication.

The term "communication" when used in this sense may seem strained, considering its customary restriction solely to verbal language. A stretching of its meaning is desirable nonetheless. It directs us away from the idea of color as symbol, and away from the problems that result from the use of this conception, toward a study of the way in which people use physical objects and their attributes in social processes. In departing from some of the traditional lines of inquiry into the nature of the physical city, we will be developing the idea that the built environment represents the material aspect of the process of human communication.

From this point of view communication includes verbal and non-verbal aspects of social interaction as well as those material objects which represent both a setting for, and artifacts of, the processes of social communication. In our previous discussion these objects were evaluated for their symbolic value to social action, not as part of a more general process of communication. This project seeks to show that so-called symbols, along with aspects of routinized social behavior, including many cultural artifacts rarely conceived of as fulfilling a symbolic or communicational function, can be assessed within a framework predicated upon a broad conception of human communication. To date the material aspects of the process of communication have not been treated adequately, either empirically or theoretically.

Communication conceived in this way offers the possibility of improving our ability to analyze human behavior in a comprehensive, contextually based manner. It promises both to contribute to social theory and to add to our understanding of the current form and historical origins of the urban built environment.

Premises of the Study

The premises for this paper's position relating urban architectonic form[1] to human communication are few but essential, in that they permit us to avoid the pitfalls of previous theory. First and most important is the premise that cultural and social systems, in all their manifestations, must be understood with special reference to the processes of communication which serve to link their components. We are interested in the way communication ties the elements of a society together, in how it fulfills the need for basic coordination and control in society. This is not to say that culture is communication, but it does imply that the two are inextricably bound together. Scientific explanation of participation in a culture requires a familiarity with the communicational conventions of the culture. This dissertation maintains that we can only know culture through its system of communication,[2] by way of the behavior and artifact that living systems continually generate, use, reuse, and discard.

The second premise is that communication must be seen pertaining to the entirety of human interaction. Verbal behavior, non-verbal behavior, kinesic cues, the use of material forms and costumes, as well as other aspects of the structure of the physical setting are all implicated in the communication process. Rather than view communication as the sequential emission, transmission, reception, and interpretation of discrete signs, symbols, and signals, this project will regard communication as a transaction or as a negotiated exchange of information, intention, and influence all closely controlled by the context within which these exchanges take place.

That we often see communication as a transmission, rather than a negotiation or exchange, may simply reflect the skill we develop for managing communicational linkages. We devote much time and effort to learning and practicing necessary conventions. These efforts provide a large reserve of common knowledge which, in common with other members of our culture, we apply to each communicative transaction. We do not always readily perceive the negotiations we participate in, nor do we always reflect upon the context which

---

1. The term architectonic is used here to denote a form generally intermediate in scale between the built environment and architectural forms. An architectonic form may be an architectural form but it can also include other aspects of material culture which would not be thought of conventionally as architectural. Architectonic forms, in this sense, can be seen as the elemental units or building blocks of the built environment.

2. Some scholars go so far as to state that to understand how a society communicates is to understand society itself. Cherry goes so far as to define society as "people in communication" (id., *On Human Communication: A Review, a Survey, and a Criticism,* 2nd ed., Cambridge, Mass.: MIT Press 1957, p. 309).

serves as the backdrop to negotiation. It is as if we walked up to people on a Chicago street and asked them why they speak English or wear a coat rather than a robe. The influence of culture as manifest in their education is so powerful yet subtle that they will be at a loss for an answer. Not only are they given to these practices but they will probably prefer them to all alternatives.

This project maintains that a communication-based analysis is the most effective way of spanning the broad range of behaviors under study. It seeks to illuminate, if only within definite limits, how our experiences with the social and built environment are related to flows of information. It takes the position that all the objects people gather around themselves, the language they use, and indeed all aspects of their behavior are better viewed as communication. Because of the inherent potential of this line of inquiry, it should come as no surprise that others have attempted communication-based analyses of the built environment; this project is not alone, broadly speaking. Even though some of the earlier work may not be well grounded in existing theory, it will probably be worthwhile to relate these traditions to the lines of thought which have led up to this project's departure.

Previous Studies of Society and Communication

In disciplines such as geography, human ecology (particularly symbolic interactionism), and sociology, premises similar to those stated above have developed from a concern with the way people relate to one another and to their social and natural environments. Yet, when scholars in these disciplines, implicitly or explicitly, have posed questions concerning the meaning, significance, and symbolic import of landscape, by no means did they always provide satisfying answers. Eventually it became apparent to some of them that the very questions they were asking about meaning and landscape were in their terms unanswerable. Even when they agreed on a definition of the term "landscape," only infrequently were they able to agree on a definition of the term "meaning." This failure goes far to explain the lack of consensus as to basic methodology that has characterized the literature addressing these questions.

It is not that the questions themselves have not been asked many times before,[3] but that their reiteration has done little more than induce a continuation of the assumptions upon which they are

---

3. For a short review of this literature see *The International Encyclopedia of the Social Sciences,* 1968 ed., s.v. "Landscape," by Marvin W. Mikesell. A lengthier review from a slightly different perspective is provided by Clarence J. Glacken, *Traces on the Rhodian Shore: Nature and Culture in Western Thought from Ancient Times to the End of the Eighteenth Century* (Berkeley: University of California Press, 1967).

based, without affording sufficient stimulus for advance. Only too
often, these efforts have resulted in a cataloguing of meanings
rather than an appraisal of the context within which symbols of
social life occur. Nonetheless, we are heirs to a number of
insights generated by these assessments, even if the conceptual
legacy is small.

People do not have the same difficulty in communicating as we
have in analyzing their behavior. They are generally ready and
accurate interpreters of their environments even if they cannot
always articulate the methods of interpretation that they employ.
They are easily able to gather and transmit information about
themselves and their situations. Some years ago certain scholars,
perceiving the weaknesses of the modes of explanation then current,
began to ask whether it might be possible to cast aside some of
their preconceptions in order to frame the relation of people to
landscape in terms of communication.[4] They saw the possibility of
uniting a mass of unassimilated observation and theory by grounding
it in a common social process. In this way, it was hoped aspects of
human territoriality, urban socio-spatial patternings, the material
costuming of culture, and many other features of the human condition
would be related to an extent not previously possible.

Support for this view of social action was afforded by studies
in material culture, the built environment, and architecture. From
these fields arose the rather naive observation that there is often
a wide discrepancy between configurations of the built environment
required for human physical survival and the totality of those that
have been created. Scholars from these fields have often wondered
why this discrepancy should exist. When their questioning was
carried to an extreme it was easy to deny the necessity for the
existing configuration of just about every element of material
culture: its corporeal dimensions, layout, material composition,
and especially what is seen, conventionally, as ornamentation. From
this perspective there is no reason for houses, factories, or
offices to take the form that they do. Any number of material
settings could serve the same purpose. Why do not people live in
tents rather than houses? Why are civic buildings, statehouses and

---

4. See for example Philip Wagner, *Environments and Peoples* (Englewood
Cliffs, N.J.: Prentice-Hall, Inc., 1972), pp. 4-6. Other writing by Wagner on
the same topic includes "Cultural Landscapes and Regions: Aspects of
Communication," *Geoscience and Man* 5 (1974):133-142. This topic is addressed
also by Edmund Leach, *Culture and Communication: The Logic by which Symbols are
Connected. An Introduction to the Use of Structuralist Analysis in Social
Anthropology* (Cambridge: Cambridge University Press, 1976); James S. Duncan, Jr.
"Landscape and the Communication of Social Identity," in *The Mutual Interaction
of People and Their Built Environment: A Cross-Cultural Perspective,* ed. Amos
Rapoport (The Hague: Mouton Publishers, 1976), pp. 391-401; and Donald W. Meinig,
ed., *The Interpretation of Ordinary Landscapes: Geographical Essays* (New York:
Oxford University Press, 1979).

courthouses, built, so often, of stone rather than of sheet metal or wood? Even modern functionalist architecture is ornamental in this sense, despite denials by its creators or rationalizations by theoretical commentators. There is a vast difference between human need as it relates to bodily survival and the preferences people express for a certain kind of house, car, or coat. Physical needs and preferences usually bear little similarity to one another.

Rapoport describes this discrepancy as a "non-critical margin."[5] If it were critical, as an airplane's wings are for flight, society could not function without it. If non-critical form is superfluous, why does it exist? Even a cursory survey reveals regularities in its patterning. Although it is easy to conclude that these forms present a wasteful use of resources, at another level they may represent an efficient means for defining and promoting social interaction. People may be using the "non-critical margin" to convey information conducive to the smooth integration of social forms. Thus, what might be seen as decoration and waste from one point of view becomes an essential feature of societal structure from another.

If we turn to linguistics, social psychology, and anthropology, we can see that the premise linking communication to artifacts and landscapes has stemmed from recognition of the close ties that exist among language, culture, and social structure.[6] Historically this recognition has served not only to inspire studies of the social foundations and dynamics of language proper, but also to provoke a chain of reasoning in which verbal language is regarded as only one form of human communication. Eventually this reasoning led to a search for comprehensive statements linking human communication in all its manifestations to culture and social structure. In turn this led to investigations into the various possible forms of human communication and served as a launching pointpoint for research into the systemic dynamics and underlying axioms invested in these modes of communication.[7] Individuals were

---

5. See Amos Rapoport, *House Form and Culture* (Englewood Cliffs, N.J.: Prentice-Hall, Inc., 1969), pp. 58-60.

6. A review of much of the anthropological literature in this area is provided by Raymond Firth, *Symbols: Public and Private* (Ithaca, N.Y.: Cornell University Press, 1973)

7. The scope of this survey can be seen to include the following sources as well as many more: Ernst Cassirer, *The Philosophy of Symbolic Forms*, vol. I: *Language* (New Haven, Conn.: Yale University Press, 1955); Colin Cherry, *On Human Communication. A Review, a Survey, and a Criticism,* 2nd ed. (Cambridge, Mass.: MIT Press, 1957); Mary Douglas, *Natural Symbols* (New York: Pantheon Books, 1970); Hugh Dalziel Duncan, *Communication and Social Order* (New York: Oxford University Press, 1962), *Symbols and Social Theory* (New York: Oxford University Press, 1969), and *Symbols in Society* (New York: Oxford University Press, 1968); Clifford Geertz, *The Interpretation of Cultures* (New York: Basic Books, 1973); Nelson Goodman, *Languages of Art: An Approach to a Theory of Symbols*, 2nd ed. (Indianapolis: Hackett Publishing Co., 1976); Louis Hjelmslev, *Language*

conceived of as communicating by word and gesture, by costume and affiliation, by patterns of consumption, through the organization of their home environment, and in many other ways.[8] Unfortunately, scholars quickly arrived at the point where the scope of their inventory exceeded the grasp of their understanding of the genesis, form, and cultural dynamics of human communication.

In brief, others have recognized communication-based analysis as an efficient way of revealing a connection between the houses people live in, the cars they drive, their vocabularies and accents, and their preferences in hobbies and foods. It is unfortunate that some of the previous investigations have been subverted by the very assumptions and interpretations that we questioned in the first chapter. In one article Eco begins by stating:

> If Semiotics, beyond being the science of recognized systems of signs, is really to be a science studying all cultural phenomena as if they were systems of signs--on the hypothesis that all cultural phenomena are, in reality, systems of signs, or that culture can be understood as communication--then one of the fields in which it will undoubtedly find itself most challenged is that of architecture.[9]

Within four pages the flaw has been introduced and Eco states:

> If architecture can, then, be considered a system of signs, the first order of business would be to characterize these signs.[10]

As we realize now, characterization of the sign is not the first order of business. It is a task that can only be undertaken much later, after we have made and analyzed a large number of observations of human action.

(Madison: University of Wisconsin Press, 1970). Gyorgy Kepes, ed., *Sign, Image, Symbol* (New York: George Braziller, 1966); John Lyons, *Introduction to Theoretical Linguistics* (Cambridge: Cambridge University Press, 1969); W. J. T. Mitchell, ed., *The Language of Images* (Chicago: University of Chicago Press, 1974); Rodney Needham, *Reconnaissances* (Toronto: University of Toronto Press, 1980) and *Symbolic Classification* (Santa Monica, Cal.: Goodyear Publishing, 1979); Erwin Panofsky, *Meaning in the Visual Arts* (Garden City, N.J.: Doubleday and Company, 1955); Valdo Pons, *Imagery and Symbolism in Urban Society* (Hull, England: Published for the University of Hull by Lowgate Press, 1975); Miles Richardson, ed., *The Human Mirror: Material and Spatial Images of Man* (Baton Rouge, La.: Louisiana State University Press, 1974); Victor Turner, *Dramas, Fields, and Metaphors: Symbolic Action in Human Society* (Ithaca, N.Y.: Cornell University Press, 1974); Paul Wheatley, *City as Symbol*, An inaugural lecture delivered at University College, London, 20 November, 1967 (London: Published for the College by H. K. Lewis, 1969); and R. R. Wohl and A. Strauss, "Symbolic Representation and the Urban Milieu," *American Journal of Sociology* 63 (March 1958):523-532.

8. Some of the best work in this area has been produced by Erving Goffman. His observations and interpretations have appeared in a number of books including *Behavior in Public Places. Notes on the Social Organization of Gatherings* (New York: Free Press, 1963); *The Presentation of Self in Everyday Life* (Garden City, N.Y.: Doubleday, 1959); and *Strategic Interaction* (Philadelphia: University of Pennsylvania Press, 1969). Other contributors to this literature include Dennis Chapman, *The Home and Social Status* (London: Routledge and Kegan Paul, 1955); James A. Davis, "Living Rooms as Symbols of Social Status: A Study in Social Judgment" (Ph.D. Dissertation, Harvard University, 1955); S. I. Hayakawa, *Symbols, Status, and Personality* (New York: Harcourt, Brace, and World, 1953); and Gregory P. Stone, "Clothing and Social Relations: A Study of Appearance in the Context of Community Life" (Ph.D. Dissertation, The University of Chicago, 1959).

9. Umberto Eco, "Function and Sign: The Semiotics of Architecture," in *Signs, Symbols, and Architecture*, eds. Geoffrey Broadbent, Richard Bunt, and Charles Jencks (New York: John Wiley, 1980), p. 11.

10. Ibid., p. 15.

For our part we must reduce our conception of communication to essentials while making sure not to carry forward discredited assumptions. There are two necessary rules for this reduction. First, communication must always be related to the context of human behavior; all of our facts concerning the use of color must be related to observations of human action. Second, we must make no presuppositions as to the divisibility of communication into verbal and non-verbal. Any and all aspects of human action must be accepted as elements in the communication process at one time or another. It is the relation between information given visually or aurally, and information communicated in other modes that presents the real challenge for the interpretor. If we separate these modes before we begin analysis we will undermine our efforts.

The Advantages of this Research Departure

There are two advantages to founding our study upon the premises and rules stated above. First, we are thereby assured that we have framed an appropriate object of study and that we are not confusing our theoretical terms with the events and actions we are using as data. Confusions of this sort in the past have beset the formulation of linguistic theory. The anticipated approach with its clear separation of theoretical terms from categories of data goes far toward assuring a viable research design.

Second, we are assured that we will be addressing questions fundamental to the understanding of social order--more specifically, questions concerning the relation of individual behavior to social action, which have been the basis of centuries of social theorizing. In earlier thinking, the issue of communication has too often been put aside while other topics have been examined in great detail. While a Marxist appraisal of social structure and its development is radically different from a Weberian analysis, neither has adequately recognized the processes of social communication which integrate a social system. However, once appropriately formulated, analysis of the coordinating and controlling functions of communication can find a place in Marxist theory. So too a place can be found in Weberian analysis, systems analysis, ecological analysis, phenomenological analysis, and other types of social analysis. Regardless of the imperatives that are seen to inform human behavior, social theories must come to an understanding of the coordinating and integrating function of communication. By extending our definition of communication so as to touch upon the broader issues of social theory we can begin to appreciate the sometimes subtle interplay of language, non-verbal behavior, and the manipulation of material artifacts. We are in a position to begin to appreciate the ways in

which social groups identify themselves and their intentions in
particular contexts by using different aspects of communication.

A Theory of Communication

We are helped in providing a theoretical outline for the work
that lies ahead by Victor Yngve's work in "human linguistics."[11] His
ideas have particular relevance for the current project because he
not only recognizes the presumptive nature of traditional linguistic
theory, but also offers a model which is capable of accounting for
human communicative phenomena in all their variety and richness.
Thus, Yngve's work is more than a critique of linguistic theory; to
his credit he also provides an alternative and better model. Owing
to its recency this model has not been thoroughly tested.[12] Its
application will be a challenge, but at least it will relieve us of
the necessity of devising our own model of human communication and
permit us to focus our attention directly on the issues at hand.

The Communicating Individual

Yngve's formulation of a theory of human communication is
grounded in the affirmation that the communicating individual must
be the object of study. The concrete physical properties of the
individual and the confirmable observations of actions undertaken by
individuals should serve as the basis for theorizing, not
aprioristic concepts such as sign, symbol, morpheme, or grammar.
Building his theory accordingly, Yngve introduces the necessary
notation and terminology, establishes suitable principles of
causality, and organizes his concepts into a structure that permits
discussion of the way individuals communicate in groups, both large
and small. Although the present project is concerned only with a
few of the elements involved in Yngve's schema, an overview of his
framework is called for.[13]

---

11. Victor H. Yngve, "Toward a Human Linguistics," in *Papers from the
Parasession on Functionalism,* Chicago Linguistics Society, April 17, 1975, eds.
Robin E. Grossman, L. James San, and Timothy J. Vance (Chicago: Chicago
Linguistics Society, University of Chicago, Department of Linguistics, 1975);
"The Struggle for a Theory of Native Speaker" in *A Festschrift for Native
Speaker,* ed. Florian Coulmas (The Hague: Mouton, 1981), pp. 29-49; "Stoic
Influences in Librarianship: A Critique," in *Libraries and Culture,* Proceedings
of Library History Seminar VI, 19-22 March 1980, Austin, Texas, ed. Donald G.
Davis, Jr. (Austin: University of Texas Press, 1981), pp. 92-105; and "Human
Linguistics: The Scientific Study of How People Communicate" (Unpublished MS,
University of Chicago, revised 1980).

12. It should also be noted that this model has not yet been fully
promulgated before the whole of its potential audience so it is too early to
assess its status with respect to competing models. Consequently, the reader
should not be misled into believing that this model is the only, or most widely
accepted, theory available. It was selected for use in the present study because
of the numerous advantages which can be realized through its application. These
advantages, which are the subject of much of the remainder of this chapter, do
not necessarily accrue to the users of other theories.

13. For more detail the reader is referred to the manuscript, Victor H.
Yngve, "Human Linguistics: The Scientific Study of How People Communicate"
(Unpublished MS, University of Chicago, revised 1980).

In the Yngvian approach to human communication the individual is modelled as a system with component properties whose state can be established through observation. The properties are those required to account for a person's communicative behavior. They take on new values through time, experience, and learning. Some change state quickly in the course of short interactions, while others, especially those dealing with the basic physical attributes and skills of the individual, can remain fixed for most of a lifetime. Through careful study of changes in the observed communicative behavior of the individual we can specify each component and its state at a given time so as to explain human interaction.

In Yngve's program of analysis, primary importance attaches to properties of four types: "basic," "procedural," "categorial," and "conditional." In figure 1, the fundamental role of these types is emphasized, while at the same time their positioning in a taxonomy of classes is made apparent. The most inclusive class, identified furthest to the right, embraces both basic and informational properties. Basic properties pertain to the equipment or mechanism that can be deployed into a configuration which supports an individual's communicational behavior. Informational properties include any and all internal regulators of communicative behavior. They must, we are to remember, operate within the constraints imposed by the basic properties.[14]

As shown in the figure, informational properties are divisible between those that, at the time of a given communicational event, are conditional and others. Conditional properties are internal states that constitute the changed situation resulting from earlier communicative behavior and that serve to trigger ensuing communicative behavior. They determine which configuration of communicative activity will be deployed relative to the context of situation and to factors internal to the individual. The other informational properties at the time of the given communicational event are repertorial, in that they comprise an inventory of available regulators.

Moving to the next level of inclusiveness, that of repertorial properties, we observe a necessary distinction between those that are procedural and those that are categorial. Procedural properties direct or guide the carrying out of communicative behavior, that is,

---

14. The basic properties might be called constitutional properties and the informational properties might be called cognitive linguistic properties, but Yngve has decided against this terminology. The distinction implied by such a terminology is only approximately correct. The distinction between basic and informational properties is not an absolute one for a given individual, but relative to the level of communicative behavior under discussion. Thus a given property of the individual may be analyzed as basic at one time and as informational at another time.

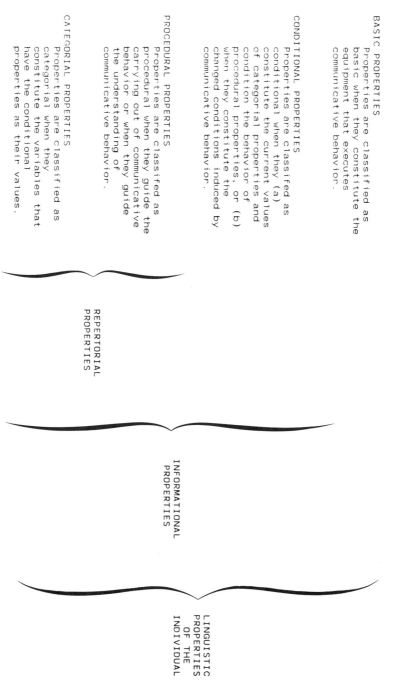

BASIC PROPERTIES
Properties are classified as basic when they constitute the equipment that executes communicative behavior.

CONDITIONAL PROPERTIES
Properties are classified as conditional when they (a) constitute the current values of categorial properties and condition the behavior of procedural properties, or (b) when they constitute the changed conditions induced by communicative behavior.

PROCEDURAL PROPERTIES
Properties are classified as procedural when they guide the carrying out of communicative behavior or when they guide the understanding of communicative behavior.

CATEGORIAL PROPERTIES
Properties are classified as categorial when they constitute the variables that have the conditional properties as their values.

REPERTORIAL PROPERTIES

INFORMATIONAL PROPERTIES

LINGUISTIC PROPERTIES OF THE INDIVIDUAL

Figure 1. Classification of the linguistic properties of the individual.

doing, saying, or understanding, given the current conditions of the individual. They are highly structured and their units or elements are called procedures. These procedures prescribe the process that deploys configurations of communicationally significant actions. There may be procedures within procedures, since the carrying out of an item of communicative behavior can often be analyzed into smaller items of communicative behavior, occurring sequentially or simultaneously. Also, there may be alternative procedures, to be carried out under similar but not identical conditions. Procedures are carried out or executed by the equipment or mechanisms labeled basic properties; when addressed by procedural properties the basic properties are allowed no option in their expression.

Finally, categorial properties provide the organization or framework for the conditions of the individual. They define the set of possible configurations of communicative activity to be deployed. (They define the possibilities for a communicative condition, even though it is the internal state of the individual at any give moment that determines which configuration is deployed). The specification contained in a procedure of the conditions under which it will be carried out is thus represented in terms of the particular values that certain relevent categorial properties must have in order for the procedure to be triggered.

What are the advantages of this formulation of the properties of the individual? First, it draws our attention away from arbitrary classifications of sensory stimuli. Sound and light waves, words and gestures--all are of much the same significance insofar as they serve to alter the conditional properties of the individual. Procedural and categorial properties can find expression in any number of modes simultaneously. In this schema language need not be separated from kinesic or gestural behavior. All three stem from a single interaction and from prescribed properties of the individual, and consequently, all are subsumed under the process of communication.

Second, this formulation forces us to frame communicative interactions discriminatingly since it specifies that the linguistic properties of the individual will vary by situation and actor. A given property of the individual, for example, may be analyzed as basic at one time and as informational at another. Further, the need for rigorous definition alerts us to the importance of mutuality. In any given interaction actors share many basic and informational properties and will be likely to respond to events in similar ways because common conditional requirements have been met. In fact, communication requires commonality of properties, even if that commonality is drastically reduced, as when individuals of different cultures and societies are able to interact even though they share nothing more than a common physiology and the same physical setting.

In most cases the context of an interaction is negotiated. Pertinent commonalities, such as shared language and experience, are normally recognized and then used by communicating individuals. In this way actors attain a certain mutuality of intent by establishing just those aspects of their commonality which contribute to their continued interaction. Other commonalities may subsequently attain significance, but only as they arise from participation in interactions themselves, or by renegotiations and redefinitions of context. The mutuality established between actors becomes the domain of control for an interaction. It is the set of possible properties which can be relied upon both to key an actor's interpretations of events and to guide that person's responses.

Establishing the domain of control of an interaction is of fundamental importance because it sets the context within which communicational reference occurs. Allusion, metaphor, anaphoric, metonymic, and other modes of reference are only possible once a domain of control has been negotiated through the mutual appraisal by communicators of significant commonalities.

It is essential to remember that all of the postulated properties of people are theoretical entities. Together they constitute a theory, model, or abstraction of the person called the communicating individual. The communicating individual is conceived as a system--not a system as usually understood in linguistics following Saussure and others, but as a dynamic-state system with inputs and outputs--in the sense customarily employed in the physical and biological sciences. Such a system is appropriate because it allows us to take into account the continually changing situational context of the individual as it affects and is affected by communicative behavior. The state of linguistic properties as it changes from moment to moment represents the situational context of that individual. What an individual understands of the communicative behavior of others depends not only on the energy input of the sounds heard and on the constitution of that individual's receptive repertory, but also on the overall state of the individual's properties at the moment of reception. This conceptualization affords a means for handling context dependence of all sorts, including so-called shifters[15] and other indexical

---

15. A shifter is a word that changes its meaning, taking its flavor from the context ("a president is young at forty, but an athlete at forty is not so

expressions, contextually relative references, tense and time
references, ellipses, and phenomena conventionally treated under
pragmatics and presuppositions. These have all been difficult
topics to understand in terms of a static sign-relation between
human actions and meaning.

A dynamic-state theory of the individual has the further
advantage of suggesting a means by which communicative phenomena can
be described and notated. Linguistic properties are seen as
attributes in respect to which individuals show similarities and
differences, one to another, and in respect to which the same
individual shows similarities and differences at various times.
Thus, with every feature of a state portrayable in terms of
similarity and difference, any state at a given time can be
represented by an array of binarily coded descriptors. These arrays
can be structured as matrices whose entries are either 0
(representing a difference) or 1 (representing an aspect of
similarity). Change is characterized by alteration in cell values.
Causation is represented either by correlations between changing
cell values in a sequence of arrays or by correlations among cell
values in coincident or synchronous arrays. In this scheme there is
no need to make judgments about affect or intent. The
characteristics of a system are completely represented by its
binarily coded descriptors.

It will be evident that, in Yngve's conception of human
communication, the theory of the individual is not a grammar of
signs and symbols internal to the individual. Instead it is a
theory of psychological and physical reality free of intervening
concepts of language and hierarchies of signs. Consequently, the
problem of the psychological reality of grammar, sign, and symbol
disappears.

The Theory of Groups

The theory of the individual, necessary as it is to a theory
of communication, is not sufficient. We also require a theory of
groups within which the social aspects of communication can be
framed. Here too Yngve is helpful, for he points out that we can
observe similarities and differences among different groups and in
the same group at different times just as we made these observations
of individuals. On the basis of these observations we can postulate
properties not only of communicating individuals but also of all
those elements of the inter-individual communication which Yngve

---

young"), or from the situation or speaker--such as the words I and me (Mario Pei,
Glossary of Linguistic Terminology, s.v. "Shifter" [New York: Columbia University
Press, 1966]).

38

terms "linkages." A linkage is a system relating any number of
communicating individuals to one another. Although linkage
properties are different from individual linguistic properties, with
which they never correspond, they are similarly structured.

We can postulate a linkage as a theoretical entity whenever we
are led by observational evidence to recognize a set of naturally
coherent and relatively self-contained communicative phenomena at
the group level. Such phenomena typically involve two or more
people, an energy flow for signalling, and possibly also objects and
environment. Persons involved in a given linkage will be called
"participants,"[16] the means for signalling will be called
"channels,"[17] objects will be called "props,"[18] and the physical
environment the "setting."[19] The participants, channels, props, and
setting of a linkage will be called the constituents of the linkage.
A linkage will also be conceived of as existing, either implicitly
or explicitly, over a definite span of time. Accordingly, linkages
will be taken as representations of particular collections of
people, means of signalling, objects, and environments that we
recognize as playing a part in communicative behavior. A naturally
coherent domain of communicative phenomena will be characterized in
terms of systemic properties at the group level, that is, properties
of the whole system.

---

16. More specifically, a participant in a linkage is an abstraction of the
communicating individual that includes just those properties of the person that
are required to account for his communicative behavior in that linkage. Since a
given individual is a participant in a number of different linkages, there will
be a number of different subsets of his linguistic properties involved in these
different linkages.

17. More specifically, a channel is a constituent of a linkage that
includes just those properties required for the physical flow of energy
associated with the signals in the linkage. There may be various kinds of
channels: there is the visual channel, concerned with the physical propagation
of light, and the auditory channel, concerned with sound and requiring the
presence of air or other medium capable of transmitting sound waves. Other
channels may appropriately be defined for the remaining senses. The concept of a
channel again helps to specify the boundaries of a linkage because it is
restricted to just the means required, thus excluding irrelevant properties of
the means of energy flow.

18. More specifically, a prop is a constituent of a linkage described by
just those properties of a physical object, analogous to the linguistic
properties of an individual, that are required for it to figure in the linkage.
Props as abstractions of physical objects can be understood in analogy to the
props in a play. Needless to say, the same object might serve as a quite
different prop in different linkages, just as the same person might be a quite
different participant in different linkages.

19. More specifically, a setting is a constituent of a linkage described
by just those properties of the physical environment, analogous to the linguistic
properties of an individual, that are required for it to figure in the linkage.
Settings and props are similar in many respects. Sometimes it may not even
matter whether a given item is classified as a prop or as part of the setting. A
prop often serves as a focus of attention for the participants or is moved or
manipulated significantly during the course of an interaction. The setting, on
the other hand, provides a relevant background, tends to be constant, and
influences the linkage usually by defining or delimiting territories, or
suggesting what communicative activities or sorts of communicative activities are
appropriate. Sometimes the dynamic properties of the setting also have to be
taken into account.

Identifying the constituents of a linkage is the first step toward understanding it as a system. The number of constituents in a linkage, and for that matter the number of participants, can be large or small. Large linkages connecting millions of participants would be needed for the study of phenomena traditionally associated with speech-communities. Intermediately sized linkages could be defined for various social, economic, political, and cultural organizations. Small linkages would be appropriate for studies of small-group and face-to-face interaction.

Another way of delimiting a linkage is to specify a definite span of time. This makes it possible to count as different linkages, for example, both a brief meeting of two friends and the entire course of their friendship. This type of definition provides the flexibility needed to delimit systems appropriate to the phenomena under consideration. If we are investigating historical change, we may postulate linkages lasting for hundreds or thousands of years. By contrast, in dealing with the development of the linguistic properties of the child in his communicative environment, linkages may be envisioned as lasting for months or years. It would also be possible to study interactions short enough to be measured in minutes, seconds, or fractions of a second.

Material Expression in Human Communication

The challenge of this project is, of course, to tie the theory of the individual and the theory of groups (as given above) to landscape and specifically to the use of color in public spaces. Can Yngve's theory of human linguistics contribute to our understanding of the physical dimension of culture? Can the urban landscape be viewed as an adjunct to, a prop for, or a mode of communication?

Any answer is likely to severely test the theory of human communication in its current state. Although large-scale structures of the cultural landscape have a place in the theory of the individual, at the same time they are far removed from the control of any given individual. The fact that explanations of the cultural landscape are contingent upon our understanding of the nature of organizations and collectivities makes the challenge of applying this schema of communication to it all the greater. It is difficult to predict whether it will be possible to make significant statements about broad, socially based linkages of a large scale--the ones that may have the most bearing on the formation of cultural landscapes--when we have not assessed even a small portion of the narrow linkages available for study.

An initial response to the challenge is to be found by inquiring how the constituents of these broad linkages (settings, participants, channels, and props) might be framed to throw light upon the interrelation of social form and landscape. Since the landscape can be regarded as a complex and multi-faceted prop, and since collectivities can assume the roles of participants, one immediate task would be to correlate role and prop in a controlled range of settings and within certain channels. In this way the investigation could be confined to the interrelation of specific independent and dependent variables.

Before we go further, we must consider props in greater detail to show how their study in linkages as broad as public displays of identity might be relevant to our understanding of narrower linkages. We must first recognize that props can be involved in all aspects of a linkage.[20] The issue is not one of how they may substitute for word or deed, but rather of how they participate in current interactions as well as influence subsequent encounters. It may be that on some occasions they also substitute for other constituents of a linkage but such substitution is a matter of affect rather than identity.

Not infrequently props serve as markers which connect various components of a single linkage or tie together elements of a set of linkages. At other times a prop functions as a sort of "memory device," and it is this role which is of particular interest to our study of landscape. As a "memory device" a prop records aspects of an interaction for future reference by linkage participants. It is the relative permanence of material artifacts which makes them so suitable for this purpose. Whereas energy transmitted in some channels dissipates rapidly, material artifacts can be appraised visually long after their significance has been established through initial interaction. However, it would be a mistake to assume that props as memory devices store information in the conventional sense of mechanisms for the storage and retrieval of information. Props in their role as memory devices are linkage specific. Only for the participants in the linkage of which the prop is a part does the prop have meaning. The prop in itself is meaningless. Props do not store information; their roles are transactional and are negotiated by linkage participants. A prop removed from one linkage may be

---

20. Of course it is apparent that depending on the linkage under consideration and its definition, material artifacts can serve as part of the setting of linkages or take on a role as prop. Though it will be interesting for future studies to examine the way material artifacts move from one to another of these roles through time, it is the use of artifact as prop which is of particular interest here. After all, it is the active use of physical objects as props which is most directly relevant to an understanding of the way landscape attains significance in human communicative interactions. Since the problem of separating foreground and background, prop and setting, can be accomplished by resolving either one, we shall concentrate on unraveling the issues of foreground and prop first.

only a part of the setting in other linkages or it may in fact "record" information of a completely different sort. The reason that items such as books are conventionally considered to be stores of information is because all literate members of a society share in the linkage which has defined the book's informational attributes. If a participant does not share in the linkage (i.e. has not been socialized to the book's language or trained in the book's use) the prop is not a memory device for that person.

This understanding of the term prop exposes the fallacy of attributing "meaning" to material objects (or the landscape) without an understanding of the interaction within which they are used. Even when we apprehend the significance of props in one interaction, it does not necessarily follow that the attributes significant to that interaction will be carried into subsequent exchanges.

The idea of the prop holds the promise of elucidating the relation between landscape and communication. The spatial arrangement of objects, objects themselves, and many other physical aspects of the built environment become recognizable as manifestations of a general process of human communication that encompasses language and nonverbal communication in an integrated whole. The physical dimension of culture as well as facets of human territoriality appear as the material aspects of communicative exchanges. These exchanges can range over the continuum of social form from expressions of identity to statements of complex goals.

It should be clear from the discussion thus far that material expression plays a special role in human communication. Its properties, particularly its relative permanence, allow it to accomplish purposes and frame interactions in ways that other actions, verbal and non-verbal, cannot. We can specify four reasons for regarding material expression as a peculiarly valuable resource for participants in a communicative transaction.

First, whereas other resources require frequent re-production for communication to occur, physical objects can be left in place so as to provide information in successive transactions without repetition of effort. For example, a stop sign replaces a traffic officer who would have to signal cars to a stop time and time again. Similarly, persons wear uniforms to define their identity without a need for verbal, repeated statement.

Second, material forms save time and effort in the information-seeking end of a transaction. When a store facade or sign lets us know what is inside the store, we are not required to go inside to gather the knowledge we need to make a decision about shopping there.

Third, material expression is sometimes more effective than other communicational means in defining qualities of interaction. Whereas in our society a person's wealth or power is sometimes difficult to declare or act out, it can be easily marked physically, as by the building of a large home of rare and expensive materials.

Fourth, material expression is capable of a long-term shaping effect. The interior design of an office, besides having aesthetic significance and a probable role to play in the establishment of identity, can enforce the the patterning of office activity over a period of many years.

Color as a Facet of Material Expression

Although it has not been mentioned directly, color is one facet of material expression. As such, it has potential as a memory device. But, even our ordinary experiences with people and environments suggest that color is not generally of overriding importance to human action. Sometimes, as in the case of traffic signals, color coding is constant and important, but there are many settings where it seems to be distributed randomly, and hence insignificantly.

The question of why color enjoys no higher level of significance than it does brings out one last point about material expression in human communication. The facets of material expression include color, size, material composition (construction materials in the case of buildings), architectural style, and other characteristics such as shape and spatial arrangement. To understand the advantages of material expression does not in itself help us to appreciate the particular facet or facets by which people choose to communicate. Sometimes we can identify a bank only by its architectural style. At other times its color is a key to identification, as can be its building materials or its siting on a particular block in a city.

To understand these details of appearance, we must consider the properties that distinguish a given facet of material expression from all others (e.g. that which sets color apart from size, siting, and so forth). It is not necessary to suppose that every facet is subject to variation at all times (even though it would be surprising if no variation took place in any one of them over the course of a large number of interactions), but it is necessary to know which facets are available in particular settings and how they can be deployed. Sometimes many facets of material expression will be included in a linkage, at other times only one will be required. In any event, the choice that is made may be expected to depend upon the properties peculiar to the facets concerned.

CHAPTER III

THE PRESENT INVESTIGATION

Color in Public Spaces

We now have at our disposal the theoretical background and
terminology required for an analysis of color use. Because we are
concerned primarily with individual behavior, we can begin the study
only when we have selected a particular linkage (or interaction).
We can then study any of the relations implied in our theory: those
involving prop, role, channel, and situation in any of the many
combinations in which they might interact consistent with that
selection.

At the present stage of research the study of props in their
complex interactions with two or three other components appears to
be beyond feasibility. Comparably unresolvable difficulties would
probably be introduced if we studied relations between either
channel and prop, or situation and prop. In the case of the
relation between channel and prop we would be forced to consider how
interactions that are bounded materially complement those bounded
either verbally and non-verbally. For the same reason it would also
be premature to study the relation of situation to prop.

We are brought, then, to the relation between role and prop.
We know that variations in role are an important feature in social
form. Let us consider how material artifacts are used to frame
roles.

For studying this relationship, a choice has been made in
favor of urban public spaces--those parts of a city's area which
permit or support the free movement of pedestrians and motorists and
are bordered by the facades of private buildings.[1] For present
purposes public spaces are an appropriate focus for investigation,
for two reasons: first, color is normally one of their salient
features; and, second, it is not difficult to locate within them a

---

1. The idea and definition of public space are issues discussed in Rob
Krier, *Urban Space* (New York: Rizzoli Publishers, 1979), pp. 15-62; Barrie
Greenbie, *Spaces: Dimensions of the Human Landscape* (New Haven, Conn.: Yale
University Press, 1981); Stanford Anderson, ed., *On Streets* (Cambridge, Mass.:
MIT Press, 1978); David K. Specter, *Urban Spaces* (Greenwich, Conn.: New York
Graphic Society, 1974); Lisa Taylor, ed., *Urban Open Spaces* (New York: Rizzoli
International, 1981); August Heckscher (with Phyllis Robinson), *Open Spaces: The
Life of American Cities* (New York: Harper and Row, 1977); and Erving Goffman,
Behavior in Public Places: Notes on the Social Organization of Gatherings (New
York: Free Press, 1963).

linkage involving only role and prop. By confining the study to a single city, we can hold the setting constant. And, if we constitute the prop (in this case the facades) as the only intermediary between social actors, the channel of interaction (confined to energy transmitted in the visual channel) will also be held constant.

Let us now specify the particular interaction between people and architectonic forms that is of interest: one in which people are drawn into and out of public space, perhaps by the desire to shop, to visit a bank, to attend church, or to patronize a hotel. In this interaction people make use of facades as they journey through city streets to avail themselves of services available behind colored architectonic facades. Organizations and individuals interact, with the facade serving as an intermediary between them. This is an interaction which, as conceived here, requires neither verbal nor non-verbal cues.

This interaction can be specified as a linkage even though it may not include the entire series of exchanges between the individual and the organization as they develop through time and involve verbal and non-verbal behavior. The concept of human communication discussed in chapter II allows us to partition behavior into appropriate units, so that there is no need to frame any further exchange (although such a course of analysis is potentially admissible). For the present, it is the initial encounter between the facade and the individual which will provide data for analysis.

We are dealing with a linkage in which there are only two roles and a single prop. One role is assigned to which ever organization we choose to consider. The other role is assumed by individuals who wish to establish contact with the organization in question. The organization's facade plays the part of the prop. Our analysis will be concerned with whether changes in a facade are contingent upon changes in associated roles. In a general sense we will be examining how organizations express their identity and values in the selection of the colors they apply to facades. We are especially interested in the way color is used to engage clients, patrons, or other users during the initial encounter that determines whether the individual will come inside or remain in public space on the street.

There is reason to believe that color will be found to vary in accordance with organizational role. This belief stems from the importance of the prop to the linkage. As an intermediary serving to initiate contact, it provides people with information about what they can expect inside, behind the facade. To be effective it must provide enough information for the individual to be able to make a decision as to whether to enter and engage in further interaction or whether to go elsewhere. If adequate information is not forthcoming, both the individual and the organization may well squander effort in unsatisfactory interactions. Customers will wander in and out of stores unable to guess from the facade the range of goods, prices, or services available within. Consequently, there are incentives for organizations to invest in facades that convey accurate information just as there are incentives for individuals to learn the conventions for interpreting facades.

By considering various properties of this linkage type we can predict some of the kinds of information which must be signalled so that interactions can flow smoothly. When studying a range of organizations such as banks, retailing establishments, hotels, restaurants, civic or governmental offices, libraries, schools, and churches, each of which is interested in involving its patrons in quite different linkages, we will expect strong functional differentiations in facades. At the same time, not all organizations of the same type cater to the same class of clientele. Restaurants, for example, offer a variety of cuisines in a variety of price ranges. Churches differ in their theologies. Hotels often specialize in attracting patrons with disparate financial resources. As a result, all these organizations have incentive to emphasize the differences in the attributes of the interactions in which they are willing to engage.

Although this does not automatically imply that color will be a dominant factor in the patterning of facades, there is no reason to assume that there will be no variation in the use of color. An absence of such variation would signify the rejection of opportunities afforded by an obvious resource. We are lead to expect color to vary in marking components of interactions by the realization that size, architectural style, and building materials vary are they are used in a similar way.

By opting for this particular interaction, one linking individuals to organizations in urban public spaces, we are opening the possibility of significant contribution to the progress of urban studies generally. There are three reasons for this. First, the front surfaces to be considered in this project comprise an important element in the physical fabric of the city. Analysis and explanation of the historical origins and present form of this fabric have long been a important theme in many domains of urban and historical geography. By examining facades in the way proposed we can readily relate the fruits of this new analysis to the findings and interpretations that have already been made.

Second, this project will be studying trips associated with economic activity, such as those for shopping or business. Since such journeys have been the subject of much study in behavioral geography, we have some assurance, again, that their analysis in the present context will make a contribution to an established body of literature.

Third, by choosing to frame interactions that must always, by definition, involve organizations, the project insures that fresh light will be thrown on another problem of enduring geographic interest, namely, the city-shaping behavior of large collectivities. By systematically applying a unifying communicational scheme to both the actions of individuals (previously approached through studies of language and face-to-face interaction) and of large collectivities, the project promises a re-conceptualization of the part played by the latter in urban life.

The Method

Development of a methodology for the project has necessitated definite decisions on these four issues:

1. What roles (i.e. organizations, by type) are to be included in the analysis?

2. How many organizations of a given type are to be analyzed?

3. How is the use of color on facades representing the organizations to be measured?

4. How are the facades to be compared statistically, with respect to color?

Resolution of these issues is reported in the course of the following discussion of the project's sampling strategy.

The Dimensions of the Sample

It is clearly not possible to analyze all the organizational roles found in even a single city. Not only are they too numerous, but they also present the prohibitive challenge of overlap, as found among multi-functional organizations and multi-purpose buildings. Fortunately, it is not be necessary to inventory every relation between role and prop in a city to establish the applicability of our conception of communication. At this stage of analysis, it is enough to investigate a small number of roles confined, for the most part, to a narrow range of purposes. However, it would be interesting to enlarge the range somewhat to include organizations catering to slightly different clienteles. At the beginning of the inquiry it is not clear whether these differences will be reflected in the facade. It might be profitable to study the facades of banks and savings-and-loan associations, as well as those of men's and women's clothing stores. We need enough organizational types to assure strong contrasts in organizational role, while including a few examples of closely related roles so as to be able to assess role-differentiaton in relation to facade coloration.

Because this is an exploratory study we will have to use our intuition to conjure up relations of possible significance, running the risk of missing some important relations, and of including some of little or no value. With continued study, a more systematic or axiomatic analysis may be expected. The organizations chosen for study can be seen as reflecting hypotheses concerning the relation of organizational type to material form, but, for the present, we will phrase them as questions rather than hypotheses, specifying the type of sample to be used for answering each question.

I.   Do facades reflect differences in the function performed by organizations? The relevant sample will include organizations which serve clearly different purposes: banks, restaurants, churches, hotels, schools, hospitals, several types of retailing establishment, and even funeral homes.

II.   If functional differentiation exists, what are its limits? Will, for example, restaurants reflect on their facades differences in their cuisines? The sample will include both banks and savings-and-loan associations, churches of several denominations, a selection of motels and hotels, and restaurants offering a broad range of cuisines.

III.   Are variations in the clientele sought by organizations having the same general function conducive to the adoption of different canons of color use? Are the facades of retail establishments which market women's clothing different from those that sell men's apparel? Do hotels that cater principally to tourists look different from those that are patronized mostly by low-income transients, or by affluent conventioneers? The sample will include a selection of men's and women's clothing stores as well as a selection of hotel types.

IV. Is the price level of an organization's goods or services reflected in its facade? The sample will include clothing stores, restaurants, and hotels spanning the price levels representative of these types of organization.

V. Is the age of an organization reflected in the coloring of its facade? The sample indicated above will be examined from this point of view.

VI. Will the size of an organization be reflected in its facade? The same sample will be examined from this point of view.

The Measurement and Transcription of Color

This project analyzed color use by means of two statistics: (1) the number of colors used on the facade, and (2) the proportion of the facade area given over to each of these colors. The spatial arrangement of colors on the facade (that is the positioning of colors in relation to one another) was not analyzed since there was no ready means of comparison. Other features associated with color, such as the reflecting efficiency of the facade surface, were also omitted from analysis. The two chosen statistics were determined for each facade in the sample by means of photographic transparencies projected onto a screen. In imitation of a method used in petrology to estimate the mineral content of rocks from thin sections, the screen upon which the photographs were projected was marked with a grid of six diagonal lines. Three were positioned in parallel at forty-five degrees to the horizontal, running from upper left to lower right, while the other three, running from lower left to upper right, were positioned in parallel at a ninety degree angle of intersection with the first three lines. All lines were calibrated in millimeters. As each slide was projected onto the screen, the length of the line-segment transecting each color noted. After the transects were measured along all six grid lines, the length of grid lines lying within the projected image of the facade was totalled, as were the line lengths for each color. These figures were used to calculate the percentage of the facade to be allocated to each color.

As an example: the length of the six grid lines transecting one particular image totalled 10004 mm, and crossed an aggregate of five color categories (the color categories will be discussed below). The line lengths lying within these colors totalled 400, 350, 100, 85, 50, and 19 mm indicating percentages on the facade of, respectively, 40, 35, 10, 8, 5, and 2.

The use of photographs to record facades is a research method that arose from compromise. It is heir to a number of deficiencies, foremost among which is the reduction of the three-dimensional character of facades to two-dimensional images. Ideally we would derive measurements of color directly from the facade or from a complete set of architectural drawings, but in practice this is impracticable. Even if permission had been granted to scale the selected facades with ladders and yardsticks, most of them would have proven to be too large for ready measurement, while architectural renderings would have been available for only a small number of buildings and then at prohibitive cost. Fortunately, it is reasonable to believe that the two-dimensional image produced photographically will not significantly distort the sampling procedure in respect of either specific colors or particular architectural shapes. Such distortion would occur only in the measurement of highly complicated color schemes. It is assumed here accordingly that such bias as there may be in this procedure, being fairly systematic and more or less constant, can be ignored.

There remain, however, three phases of the photo-transcription process in which error can be introduced. These errors can be minimized or compensated for. First, facades vary greatly in size. Some are so large that it is impossible to record them in their entirety in any one picture. This is particularly true when a facade extends along more than one street. (We are, of course, interested only in facades which face public spaces rather than those at the rear or side.) Although it would be possible to obtain and analyze a series of photographs spanning the entire facade, such a process would be unjustifiably time consuming, especially if there were reason to believe that a single carefully chosen picture could yield the same information, as proved to be the case in the present study.

In a test of ten large facades, each was first transcribed using as many as six photographs. As a standard of comparison single photographs of the same facades were analyzed separately. In no case did the statistics produced by the two procedures differ by more than ten percent. The large facades were remarkably homogeneous, even those constructed in the earlier decades of this century that incorporated distinct styles of facing (and hence different colors) at successive elevations. The facades of these buildings were typically faced with gray or brown stone on the lower three to five floors as well as on the two to four floors at and immediately beneath the cornice, while the rest of the structure was faced with dark red or brown brick.

It was decided that, however large a facade might be, its color would be sampled with one photograph, but that the selection of the picture would be standardized. Because variation in color in smaller facades is designed to engage the vision of people walking at street level, the photographic record was restricted to the first forty feet of facade height. Moreover, because we were interested in interactions which draw people into buildings, the photographs were always centered on an entrance. When a building had more than one entrance, only the main one was photographed.

The second source of potential error lay in variations in the angle of the facade to, or its distance from the camera.[2] Unfortunately there was no means for avoiding such variations. To minimize their effect, all photographs were taken within a thirty to sixty degree angle of the primary plane of the facade, centered on the main entrance. Where adequate coverage was a problem, the distance between facade and camera was increased to include up to forty feet of height and as much of the surface of the facade as this restriction permitted. Variations in camera positioning occurred throughout the photographing of the sample population, and had to be taken into account as the results of the analysis were weighed and compared. It must be realized that these variations affected only one of the two statistics gathered in the study, namely the percentages of facade area devoted to particular color categories. It did not significantly affect the statistic which recorded the number of colors on the facade.

The third and final question concerns color reproduction: do the photographs comprise an adequate record of the colors used on the facades? As a test, a number of projections from slides were compared with color inventories prepared in the field from the facades. No significant differences between these records were discovered. Nonetheless, precautions were taken during the photographic sampling to prevent the introduction of errors of this type. Only one camera and one type of film (Kodak Ektachrome 64 [KR135-36], ASA 64) were used. All of the film was processed by an authorized agent of its manufacturer and handled by a single dealer. To minimize the effect of varied lighting conditions and the problem of shadow, photographs were taken between 10:00 AM and 2:00 PM. No photographs were taken on overcast or rainy days. All of the

---

2. The major source of this error, again, resides in the difficulty of recording a three-dimensional object on a two-dimensional slide. Many facades make use of signs which project at a right angle to their main face, particularly near entrances and close to street level, the areas of the facade with which we are most concerned.

photographs were taken between June 26, 1981 and July 31, 1981 when vegetation was in its summer luxuriance.

As to error that might be introduced by the grid-linear method of measurement, convincing confirmation of accuracy had already come from petrology, the discipline from which the method was adopted. During the development of this method, petrologists asked themselves whether it yielded satisfactorily accurate estimations of mineral content in specimen cross sections. Statisticians were able to prove that the grid-linear measurements strongly converged on an accurate estimate of area.[3]

Direct confirmation of the accuracy of the method was provided by some empirical comparisons undertaken during the early stages of this project. Color prints on paper were compared with color slides. The former were cut into small pieces, according to color. The pieces were grouped by color category and weighed. Percentages of color composition were calculated by dividing the weight of paper covering the entire facade (calculated by summing the weights of all the color fragments) into the weight of the color fragments of a particular category.[4] (The method assumed that photographic paper is uniform in its weight-to-area ratio.) No difference was observed between transcriptions made from prints by the cut-and-weigh method, and those made by applying the grid-linear technique to projected slides.

One last topic relating to color as recorded by photographs had to be addressed. Given the sometimes subjective nature of color evaluations, what standards were to be used to identify and notate colors? This question resolved into a choice from among already-established systems of color notation, each with its standards of reference,[5] including a color atlas and a dictionary. One can match a color against samples found in the atlas and then use the dictionary to determine that color's notation or name in a number of different systems.

The system selected as a basis for our analysis is one developed by A. H. Munsell.[6] It arranges the three attributes of

3. F. Chayes, "Looking Through Rocks," in *Statistics: A Guide to the Unknown*, 2nd ed., eds. Erich L. Lehmann and Judith M. Tanur (San Francisco: Holden-Day, 1972), pp. 362-371.

4. This method of analysis is sometimes used in geographic and geologic study to estimate the pedological or stratigraphic character of a region. A map of the soils or stratigraphy is cut up, the pieces grouped and weighed, and estimates of areal character are calculated from the resulting statistics.

5. For examples consult the chapter on color systems in Martina Duttmann, Friedrich Schmuck, and Johannes Uhl, *Color in Townscape* (San Francisco: W.H. Freeman and Co., 1981), pp. 59-83.

6. Albert H. Munsell, *A Color Notation*, 13th ed. (Baltimore, Md.: Munsell Color Company, 1979). For a history of the development of this system see Dorothy Nickerson, "History of the Munsell Color System, Company, and

color, hue (the chromatic color category), value (the lightness or darkness of a color), and chroma (the strength or weakness of a color),[7] in orderly scales for the accurate specification and description of color under standard conditions of illumination and viewing. The Munsell scales for hue, value, and chroma can be visualized in terms of a color solid, or color space as in figure 2. The neutral value scale, graded in equal visual steps, from black at the bottom to white at the top, forms the central vertical axis. The hue scale is organized in equal visual steps around the neutral axis. Chroma scales radiate in equal visual steps from the neutral axis outward to the periphery of the color space. The color space defined by the Munsell color solid conforms, roughly, to the present limits of absolute saturation in natural pigment and dye materials. A vertical cross-section of the color solid is displayed in figure 3 together with the ISCC-NBS color names (see below) associated with its various sub-areas. The atlas used for comparison during the present analysis is an adaptation of the Munsell notation published by the Inter-Society Color Council in conjunction with the National Bureau of Standards, known as the ISCC-NBS standard. The names of its colors can be readily converted to Munsell notation through the use of the ISCC-NBS dictionary of color names.[8]

  With the matter of color standards settled, two procedural

Foundation: Part I," *Color Research and Application* 1 (Spring 1976):7-10, and "History of the Munsell Color System, Company, and Foundation: Part II," *Color Research and Application* 1 (Summer 1976):69-77.
  The Munsell notation system is useful whenever color communication and specification are necessary. The equally spaced color scales provide a tool for expressing the perceived color of an object and the color differences among a group of objects. The notation is univerally used in research studies on the physics and psychology of color and many government and industrial color specifications are cast in terms of Munsell notation. The American National Standards Institute and The American Society for Testing and Materials also have incorporated the Munsell notation in their standards. The Inter-Society Color Council and the National Bureau of Standards use it to specify color-name limits in the ISCC-NBS Method of Designating Color. The Japanese Industrial Standard for Color is similarly based on the Munsell notation, and The British Standards Institute uses the notation to designate standard paint colors. The German Standard Color System goes so far as to provide a Munsell notation for each of its 585 samples. The simplicity and flexibility of the Munsell system allow for countless applications.

  7. The hue of a color (H) indicates its relation to an equally spaced visual scale of 100 chromatic categories. There are ten major hues (five principal and five intermediate) positioned ten hue steps apart within the scale. The hue notation in general use is based on the ten major hue names: Red, Yellow-Red, Yellow, Green-Yellow, Green, Blue-Green, Blue, Purple-Blue, Purple, and Red-Purple.
  The value of a color (V) indicates the degree of lightness or darkness of a color in relation to a neutral gray scale, which extends from absolute black to absolute white. The value symbol 0/ is used for absolute black; the symbol 10/ is used for absolute white. The symbol 5/ is used for the middle gray and for all chromatic colors that appear half way in value between absolute black and absolute white.
  The chroma of a color (C) indicates the degree of departure of a given hue from a neutral gray of the same value. The scales of chroma extend from /0 for a neutral gray to /10, /12, /14, or further, depending upon the strength (saturation) of the sample to be evaluated. A color classified popularly as "scarlet" might have a chroma as strong as /12 or as vivid as /16, while another color of the same hue and value, classified popularly as "rose," might have a chroma as weak (grayed) as /4.
  The complete Munsell notation for a chromatic color is written symbolically as H V/C. For a sample of "scarlet" the complete notation might be

53

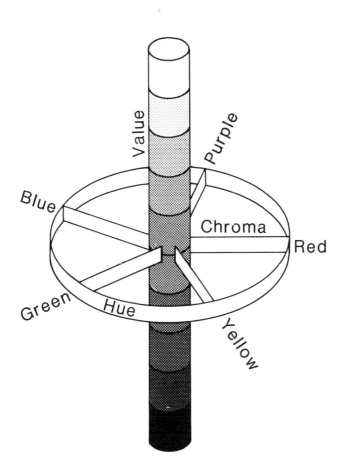

(a) The dimensions

Figure 2. The Munsell color solid.

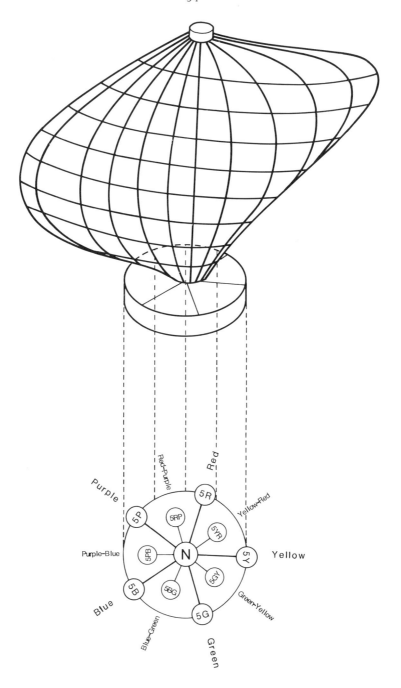

(b) The solid with Hue designations.

55

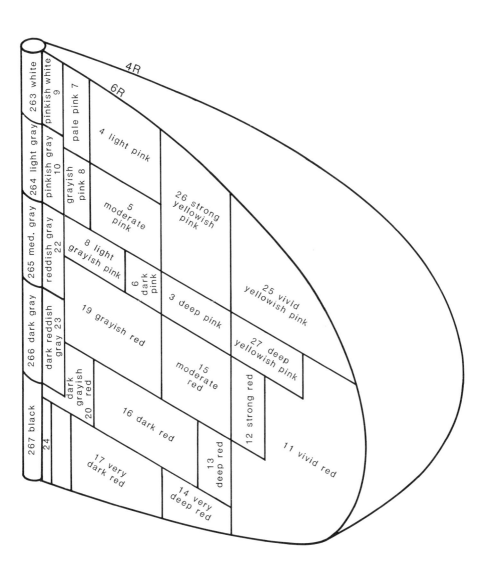

FIGURE 3: A Section of a Color Solid Partitioned According to the ISCC-NBS System of Notation.

problems were still outstanding. First, how were colors relevant to human behavior in public spaces to be defined over the enormous known range of human differentiation (more than a million distinctions)? Second, how were we to insure that identification of the defined colors, working from photographs, would be accurately executed?

The structure of the Munsell system was, in itself, of help with the first problem. Not only does it reduce the continuum of human color perception to just over 1500 designations (among which further interpolation could be made), but it also allows one to devise abridged sets of standards to meet the requirements of particular research problems.[9] The prospects for a special abridgment suitable to the transcription of colors found in public spaces appeared promising from the outset. An abridgement was, in fact, developed from preliminary field surveys.

During these surveys it became evident that far fewer color distinctions would be needed than are presented in the Munsell system. Very few facades use colors in the Red-Purple, Purple, and Purple-Blue ranges. The distinctions needed in the Red, Yellow, Blue, and Green hues are no more than simply light, middle, and dark (by chroma) and vivid as against non-vivid (by value). Moreover, a large portion of the urban fabric is cast in shades of brown, a color which spreads across the lower chroma and lower values of the Red-Yellow and Yellow hue ranges. In the end, observation suggested that most of the social relations important to this study could be captured using no more than about thirty color categories from the Munsell system. Of its ten principal hues, five (Red, Yellow, Green, Blue, and Purple) were retained together with the achromatic (white to black) neutral-value scale. One intermediate hue, Yellow-

---

5R 4/16, while the notation for a sample of "magenta" might be 4RP 3/8. When a finer division is needed for any of the attributes, decimals are used; for example: 3.8R 5.4/10.6.

The notation for a neutral (achromatic) color is written: N V/. The notation for a sample of black, a very dark neutral, might be N 1/; the notation for a sample of white, a very light neutral, might be N 9/, while the notation for a gray, visually half way between these two, would be N 5/.

The chroma symbol /0 may be included in the notation for neutral colors but is customarily omitted. Blacks, grays, and whites of chroma weaker than /0.3 are customarily notated as neutrals. If a more precise notation is required, the form used is N V/(H,C). That is, the symbol for one of the ten major hues is combined with that of the chroma. Thus, a light gray of a slightly yellowish appearance might have a notation of N 8/(Y,0.2). It is, of course, also correct to use the regular H V/C form to describe all colors, using N V/0 for absolute neutrals.

8. U.S., Department of Commerce, National Bureau of Standards, *Color: Universal Language and Dictionary of Names,* by Kenneth L. Kelly and Deane B. Judd, (Washington, D.C.: Government Printing Office, 1976).

9. Abridged sets of standards have been devised to meet the specific requirements of certain research fields. Plant-tissue and soil-color collections are used, for instance, by agronomists, biologists, archaeologists, and geologists. Other charts and special scales are used in television, photography, microfilming and illuminating engineering, for the grading of raw and processed foods, and for the specification of safety colors in industry.

Red (orange), was retained. A scale sensitive to variations in hue, value, and chroma among shades of brown was added. Within the achromatic and brown scales distinctions were made principally on the basis of chroma. In the other hue ranges, three categories were used to characterize colors of similar value but of varying chroma. A fourth category was added to each hue range for colors of high value, regardless of chroma. Figure 4 displays a section of the Munsell color solid in the Red hue range to demonstrate the manner in which the solid was partitioned for application in the present study. Table 1 lists the specifications for this study's abridgment of the entire Munsell color solid together with the adopted color nomenclature.

There were two deviations from the application of this identification system. A preliminary survey of color in public spaces suggested that exposed metals were as important to this analysis as any other major category. Although they could be described in terms of the Munsell system, a decision was made to assign them a separate standing. Accordingly, three metallic tones were recognized: silver-steel-aluminum (the gray metals), gold-brass-bronze (the yellow and yellow-brown metals), and copper (a dark-brown metal usually covered with a light green oxide patina). The preliminary survey also suggested that colored lights on facades should be classified independently. Thus, red, yellow, orange, purple, white, blue, and green lights were recorded as categories in their own right (e.g. "Red Light" instead of "Vivid Red").

As to the problem of accuracy, introduced on an earlier page, a sound and consistent procedure for transcribing from slides was obviously called for. It was necessary to insure, for example, that for a color on a facade to be classified "Light Red" its attributes would always meet the specifications for that category as defined in table 1. To minimize error arising from imperfect discrimination among colors on the boundaries of these categories, the transcription from slides was always effected with the aid of the ISCC-NBS centroid color charts.[10] These charts took the form of atlas leaves upon which were printed color chips meeting the required standards and tolerances of the Munsell system.

To reduce the likelihood of error or bias originating in the transcriber, a random sample of the transcriptions were repeated by another person. Moreover, periodically some slides were retranscribed to insure that the investigator's evaluation of color boundaries was not changing as the analysis progressed.

---

10. U.S., Department of Commerce, National Bureau of Standards, *Inter-Society Color Council and National Bureau of Standards (ISCC-NBS) Color-Name Charts Illustrated with Centroid Colors* (Washington, D.C.: Government Printing Office, 1976).

58

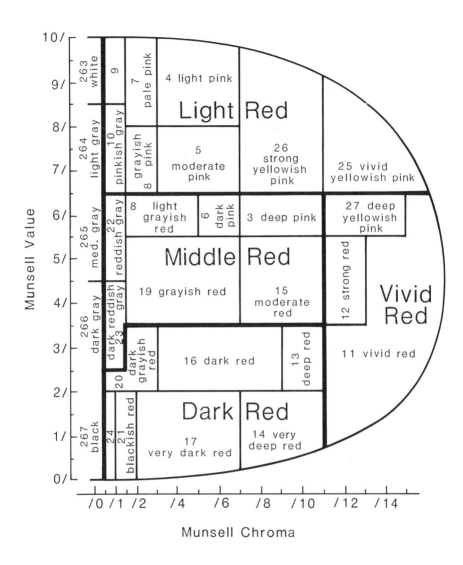

FIGURE 4: One Section of a Color Solid (with ISCC-NBS color labels) Partitioned According to the Specifications of the Present Study.

TABLE 1

THE DIVISION OF THE MUNSELL COLOR SOLID ADOPTED FOR THIS PROJECT

COLOR	HUE	VALUE	CHROMA
White		8/-10/	/0-/1
Light Gray		6/-8/	/0-/1
Dark Gray		4/-6/	/0-/1
Black		0/-3/	/0-/1
Light Red	5RP-10R-2YR	6.5/-10/	/0-/14
Vivid Red	5RP-10R	1/-6.5/	/10.5-/14
Middle Red	7RP-10R	2.5/-6.5/	/1-/10.5
Dark Red	7RP-10R	0/-3.5/	/1-/10.5
Light Orange	2YR-1Y	8/-10/	/1-/10
Vivid Orange	2YR-1Y	4.5/-10/	/10-/15
Middle Orange	2YR-1Y	6.5/-8/	/3-/10
Dark Orange	2YR-1Y	4.5/-6.5/	/3-/12
Beige	2YR-4Y	5/-7.5/	/.5-/4.5
Light Brown	2YR-4Y	4/-5/	/1-/6
Middle Brown	2YR-4Y	2.5/-4.5/	/1-/12
Dark Brown	2YR-4Y	0/-2.5/	/1-/12
Light Yellow	1Y-10Y	8/-10/	/1-/8
Vivid Yellow	1Y-10Y	5.5/-10/	/8-/14
Middle Yellow	1Y-10Y	6.5/-8/	/2-/8
Dark Yellow	1Y-10Y	5.5/-6.5/	/2-/8
Light Green	1GY-5BG	6.5/-10/	/1-/6.5
Vivid Green	1GY-5BG	3/-10/	/6.5-/14
Middle Green	1GY-5BG	3.5/-6.5	/1-/6.5
Dark Green	4Y-5BG	0/-4.5/	/0-/12
Light Blue	5BG-7PB	5.5/-10/	/1-/8.5
Vivid Blue	5BG-7PB	3/-10/	/8.5-/14
Middle Blue	5BG-7PB	3/-5.5/	/1-/8.5
Dark Blue	5BG-7PB	0/-3/	/1-/12
Light Purple	7PB-5RP	5.5/-10/	/1-/8.5
Vivid Purple	7PB-5RP	0/-5.5/	/1-/8.5
Dark Purple	7PB-7RP	1/-8.5/	/8.5-/14

R: Red
YR: Yellow-Red
Y: Yellow
GY: Green-Yellow

BG: Blue-Green
PB: Purple-Blue
RP: Red-Purple
P: Purple

Note: In a few cases the specifications of the color categories given in this table overlap in one or another of its three dimensions. This resulted from the specification of irregularly shaped ISCC-NBS color pockets by recourse to the Munsell system. The actual investigation was carried out using detailed color charts free of any classificatory ambiguity. This charts, too numerous to be listed here, are only approximately summarized in this table.

The Sample

Size

Now we must turn to the question of the size of the sample. Would the sample, to serve as an adequate basis for generalization, necessarily include all organizations of a given type or class existing in a particular city, or would a selection, perhaps rather small, be sufficient?

Lacking guidance from previous research on color in public spaces, and finding no justification for attempting a solution from theoretical considerations alone, we approached the question as an essentially empirical one, calling for the calculation of variance within classes of the experimental sample. Ideally, there would be a large enough number of organizations in the sample to insure that variation in color use by type would be stable or constant; the addition of another organization to a class would not change the distribution of color use in that class. In the calculations that were made, each distribution was, of course, a series of averages for a color category taken from the data available for a given organizational type. We would have wished to create a situation where, for a particular type, color use would stabilize at, say, forty percent of the total facade area in black, thirty percent in white, ten percent in vivid red, ten percent in light gray, five percent in light yellow and five percent in light brown. If such stability could not be achieved, it would be desirable to restrict change in any particular color category, resulting from the addition of organizations, to less than five percent.

At an early stage of study a trial assessment of the number of organizations required to achieve this degree of stability was undertaken. Composite color distributions were calculated using first two, then three, then more of the prepared transcriptions until the requisite degree of convergence was achieved. For certain types of organization, sufficient convergence took place after only ten distributions had been averaged. This was true for religious and educational organizations, public institutions, and banks. The addition of more organizations did not change the distribution. For the least convergent organizations, stability was achieved using between twenty-five and thirty cases.

As a result of this kind of empirical test, it was possible to establish a standard of sample size; it was found that thirty organizations of a given type or class would be sufficient. In our calculations, when a color distribution converged before thirty transcriptions had been inspected, no more organizations were added to that particular subsample. Anywhere between ten and thirty organizations of each subsample were required. Occasionally more than the required minimum were included in the statistical analysis simply because they were available. This was so, for instance, when the facades of banks were compared with those of savings-and-loan associations for functional differentiation by color use. Color use on both of these facade types converged rapidly so that only about a dozen of each were required. However, because we were also interested in studying the relation between organizational size and facade coloration, a relation which required at least forty facades of each type, forty were collected and analyzed.[11]

The Universe

The sample of organizations and facades used in the present study was drawn from the total represented within the city limits of Chicago, Illinois. Collection began at the center of the city, where there was the greatest concentration of the types of organization predesignated for the study. Once Chicago's central district had been fixed upon as the focus of this decidely exploratory analysis, two problems emerged: first, when a superabundance of organizations of a given type existed in Chicago's central district, how were the relatively few required for study to be selected; and second, when too few organizations of a given type were available, how was the study area to be expanded to include the necessary number?

As a basis for solution to both these problems, an inventory of each type and class of organization in the central area was compiled. It was drawn from field observation as well as general guide books, the telephone directory, business guides, and local magazines. When, for example, it became apparent that there were almost five times as many low-cost restaurants in the central district as would be needed, a random, twenty-percent sample was drawn from their total number.[12] When there were not enough organizations of a given type or class, as happened with churches, for example, the study area was systematically enlarged until a sufficiency had been enclosed. Guide books and local magazines were particularly useful at this point.[13] Enlargements always involved additions, of approximately equal area, to the immediate north, west, and south of the central district. Figure 5 exhibits the final study territory. Seventy percent of the organizations were drawn from a primary study area lying between Lake Michigan on the east, the branches of the Chicago River on the west, 12th Street on the south, and Division Street (1200 north) on the north. The area from which the complete sample was drawn extended further to the north, west, and south, as shown.

---

11. To study the relationship between organizational size and facade coloration banks and savings-and-loan associations were grouped into four size categories each of which required the assessment of ten to twelve facades.

12. This pattern of sampling occurred during the photographic field sessions. Since every street in the central study area was walked as a transect to its entire length, it was sufficient to photograph every fifth low-cost restaurant. The choice of transects was determined at random.

13. These included *Chicago Magazine,* April, May, June, and July, 1981, (Chicago: WFMT, Inc.); The American Automobile Association, *Tourbook: Illinois, Indiana, Ohio* (Falls Church, Va.: The American Automobile Association, 1981); *Key Magazine,* June and July, 1981, (Chicago: This Week in Chicago, Inc.); Rand McNally and Company, *Mobil Travel Guide: Great Lakes Area, 1981* (Chicago: Rand McNally and Co., 1981); Sherman Kaplan, *Best Restaurants: Chicago and Suburbs, Revised and Expanded* (San Francisco: 101 Publications, 1979); and *Where Magazine: Chicago* June and July, 1981, (Chicago: Media Networks, Inc.).

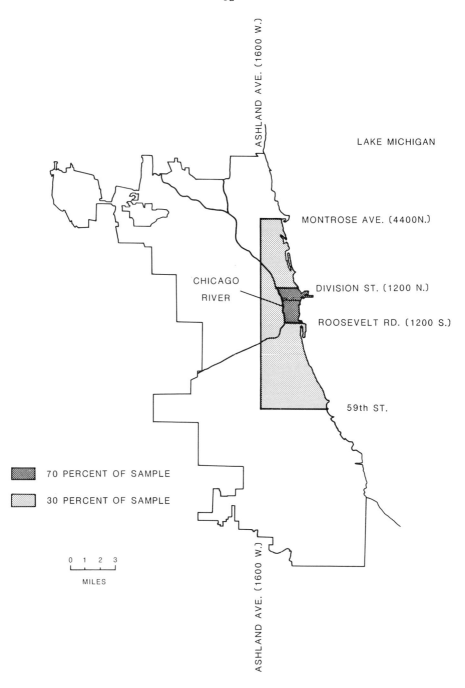

FIGURE 5: The Study Area in Chicago, Illnois.

Statistical Comparisons

As we have seen, this project's method of photo-transcription generated two classes of data: the total number of colors used on a facade (regardless of the area occupied), and the percentage of facade area given over to each color category. The first class of data were evaluated by one-way Analysis of Variance (ANOVA) techniques, the second by two-way ANOVA techniques.[14] In the former, variances in the number of colors used on facades were compared according to the type or class of organization they represented. In the latter, the color variable was employed to structure a comparison across organization types or classes of the recorded percentages.

The same techniques were further applied to probe more deeply into color use on facades. It was discovered, for instance, that a strong relation existed between restaurants of various price levels both the number of colors used on the facade and the percentages of facade area covered by each color. More expensive restaurants used fewer colors and arranged them over more varied proportions of their surface areas than did lower priced restaurants. And, it was further discovered that the bases of difference involved a total of only a very few colors. All classes of restaurant employed black and white in much the same way, but their use of vivid reds and yellows differed significantly, so much so that these colors clearly qualified as diagnostic indicators or predictors of organizational form.

---

14. Details of the theory and method of ANOVA statistical techniques can be obtained from H. D. Brunk, *An Introduction to Mathematical Statistics,* 2nd ed. (Lexington, Mass.: Xerox College Publishing, 1975), pp. 373-390; and from Hubert M. Blalock, Jr., *Social Statistics,* 2nd ed. (New York: McGraw-Hill Book Co., 1972), pp. 317-357.

CHAPTER IV

THE RESULTS OF THE INVESTIGATION

The relationships introduced in chapter III will now be considered in the light of the statistics generated in the course of their study. In each case we will consider first the number of colors used on the facade, then the percentages of facade area assigned to the various color categories, and, finally, other findings pertaining to color use. By way of introduction to the investigation, table 2 presents the facade sample as distributed among organizations, by type and sub-type.

Organizational Type and Color Use

All the organizational types included in the survey, specifically banks, restaurants, churches, hotels, educational institutions, hospitals, retail establishments, funeral homes, and public/governmental institutions, were incorporated in the later analysis. In the case of restaurants, banks, hotels, and retail establishments, where the sample included more than thirty instances, thirty examples were selected at random for analysis. In dealing with hospitals, funeral homes, educational institutions, and civic institutions, it proved practicable to limit the number of instances for analysis to fifteen, since the color schemes of these organizations had converged by that point. The analysis proceeded as follows.

First, it was asked whether organizational function was related to the number of colors used on facades. Figure 6 graphs the average number of colors used by each type of organization. Testing by a one-way ANOVA model revealed that their were significant statistical differences in the number of colors used among the various types (table 3). Second, the same sample of facades was analyzed for the proportion of the various colors used. Figures 7, 8, 9, 10, 11, 12, 13, 14, 15, and 16 are graphs of average color composition for each of ten organizational types. Two-way ANOVA analysis (table 3) showed that there was a significant difference in proportions of color use by organizational type.

TABLE 2

SAMPLE SIZE BY ORGANIZATIONAL TYPE AND SUB-TYPE

TYPE OF ORGANIZATION	NUMBER OF FACADES
Banks (total)	49
By Age	
1. Age < 43 years	9
2. 43 ≤ Age < 65 years	11
3. 65 ≤ Age < 87 years	10
4. Age ≥ 87 years	6
By Size (Assets in thousands)	
1. Size < $724,570	8
2. $724,570 ≤ Size < $1,131,490	8
3. $1,131,490 ≤ Size < $1,538,410	13
4. $1,538,410 ≤ Size < $1,945,330	12
Savings-and-Loan Associations (total)	36
By Size (Assets in thousands)	
1. Size < $183,360	9
2. $183,360 ≤ Size < $609,380	12
3. $609,380 ≤ Size < $1,035,400	8
4. $1,035,400 ≤ Size < $1,441,420	7
Churches (total)	99
By Denomination	
1. Roman Catholic	15
2. Greek Orthodox	8
3. Lutheran (ALC)	12
4. Baptist	12
5. United Methodist	11
6. Jewish	8
7. Presbyterian	12
8. Christian Science	13
9. Unaffiliated	8
Restaurants (total)	191
By Price Level	
1. Price < $5.99	45
2. $5.99 ≤ Price < $12.07	40
3. $12.07 ≤ Price < $18.15	40
4. Price ≥ $18.15	39
By Cuisine	
1. Chinese	19
2. Japanese	12
3. Greek	11
4. Italian	15
5. Mexican	19
6. French	13
7. Soulfood	12
8. Seafood	12
9. Steakhouses	15
Retail Establishments (total)	114
By Commodity	
1. Clothing	70
2. Food	15
3. Drugstores	14
4. Hardware	15
By Gender-Defined Clientele (Clothing)	
1. Female	35
2. Male	41
By Price Level (Clothing)	
1. Lowest Price	24
2. Intermediate Price	24
3. Highest Price	22
By Age	
1. Age < 16 years	22
2. 16 ≤ Age < 30 years	18
3. 30 ≤ Age < 44 years	19
4. Age ≥ 44 years	12

TABLE 2-continued.

Educational Institutions (total)	35
By Type	
1. Primary	11
2. Secondary	12
3. College/University	12
Funeral Homes (total)	15
Hospitals (total)	12
Public/Governmental Institutions (total)	13
Hotels (total)	82
By Price Range	
1. Price < $13.07	14
2. $13.07 ≤ Price < $39.28	29
3. $39.28 ≤ Price < $65.49	20
4. $65.49 ≤ Price < $91.70	14
By Size	
1. Size < 482 rooms	21
2. 482 ≤ Size < 997 rooms	15
3. Size ≥ 997 rooms	8
By Age	
1. Age < 26 years	12
2. 26 ≤ Age < 45 years	12
3. Age ≥ 45 years	12
Motels (total)	16

TABLE 3

COLOR USE BY ALL ORGANIZATIONAL TYPES

Source	df	SS	F value	Pr > F
1. Number of Color Categories				
Model	16	602.43	10.71	<.001
Error	465	2339.24		
Total	481	2941.67		
2. Percentage of Facade Devoted to the Color Categories				
Model	16	158826.15	71.31	<.001
Error	11808	1636875.24		
Total	11824	1345701.39		

Organizational Type and Color Use: Limits and Refinements

Not only did our analysis uncover a statistically significant
relation between function and color use when facades for individual
types were compared with facades for all types, it also revealed a
marked similarity among certain organizations, in both the number
and proportions of colors used. For example, banks, public
institutions, churches, and funeral homes showed no significant
difference in the way that they employed colors (table 4).
Hospitals, educational institutions, and hotels also tended to share
a common color scheme (table 5), although this relation was not as
strong as the previous one. Restaurants and retail establishments
also were found to be quite similar (table 6). Conversely, when the
organizations were regrouped into three categories to reflect these

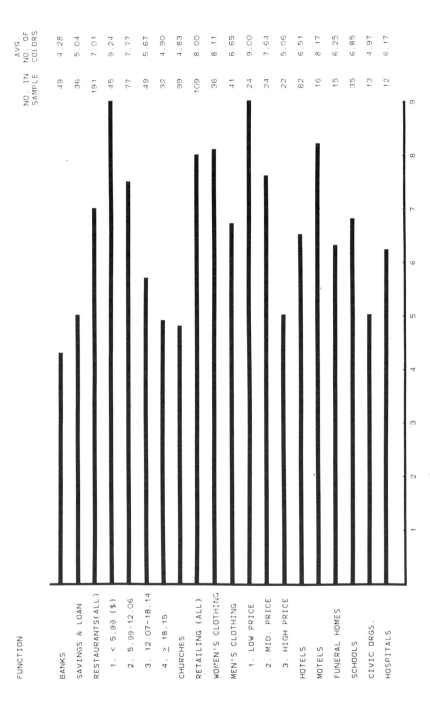

Figure 6. Number of colors used by organizational type.

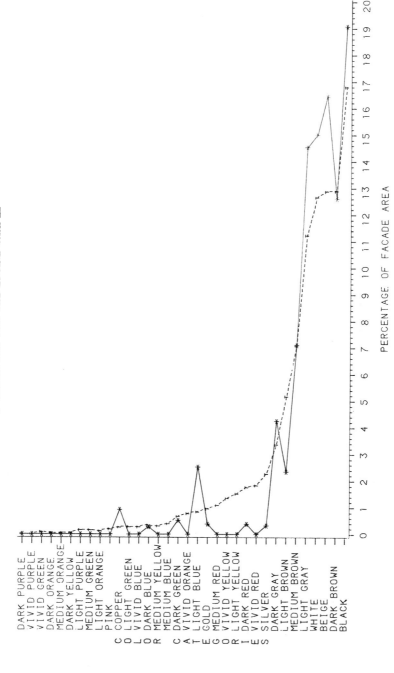

Figure 7. Color use by banks.

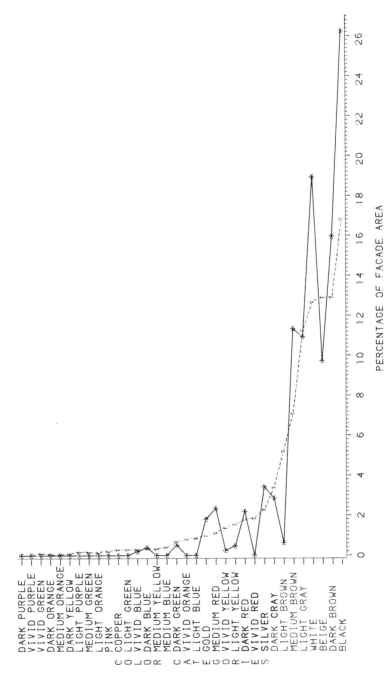

*=COLOR USE BY SAVINGS-AND-LOAN ASSOCIATIONS
T=COLOR USE FOR THE ENTIRE SAMPLE

DARK PURPLE
VIVID PURPLE
VIVID GREEN
DARK ORANGE
MEDIUM ORANGE
DARK YELLOW
LIGHT PURPLE
MEDIUM GREEN
LIGHT ORANGE
PINK
C COPPER
O LIGHT GREEN
L VIVID BLUE
O DARK BLUE
R MEDIUM YELLOW
MEDIUM BLUE
C DARK GREEN
A VIVID ORANGE
T LIGHT BLUE
E GOLD
G MEDIUM RED
O VIVID YELLOW
R LIGHT YELLOW
I DARK RED
E VIVID RED
S SILVER
DARK GRAY
LIGHT BROWN
MEDIUM BROWN
LIGHT GRAY
WHITE
BEIGE
DARK BROWN
BLACK

PERCENTAGE OF FACADE AREA

0   2   4   6   8   10   12   14   16   18   20   22   24   26

Figure 8. Color use by savings-and-loan associations.

71

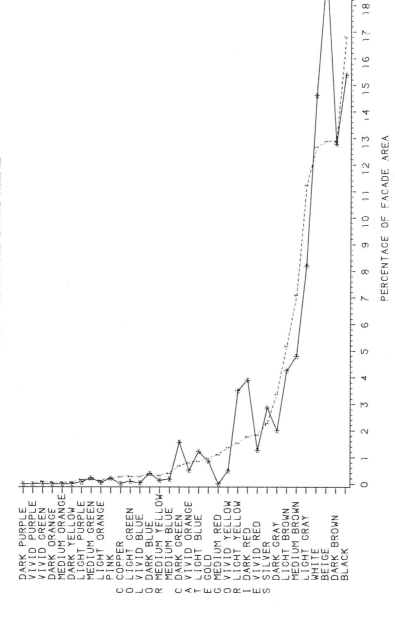

Figure 9. Color use by hotels.

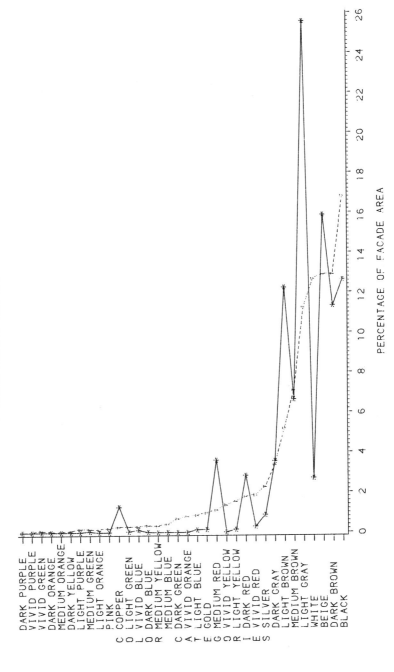

*=COLOR USE BY CHURCHES
T=COLOR USE FOR THE ENTIRE SAMPLE

Figure 10. Color use by churches.

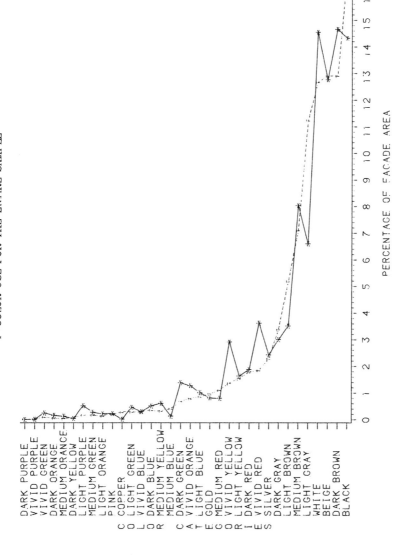

Figure 11. Color use by restaurants.

74

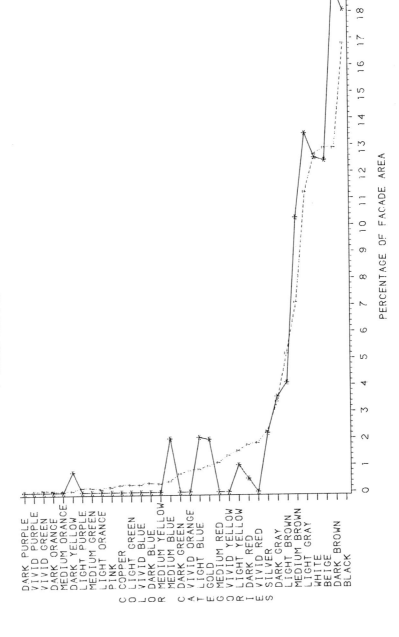

Figure 12. Color use by educational institutions.

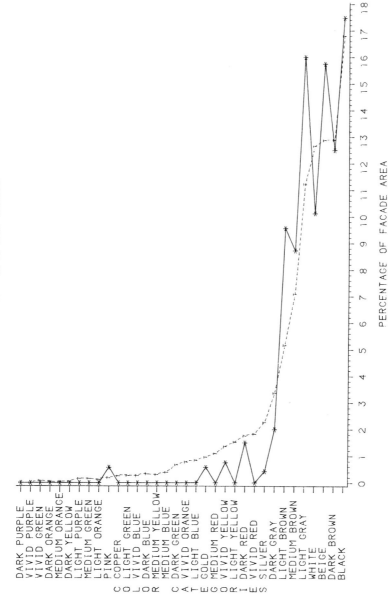

Figure 13. Color use by public and governmental institutions.

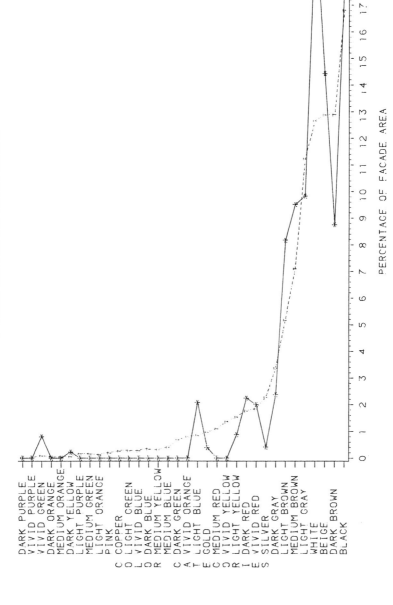

*=COLOR USE BY HOSPITALS
T=COLOR USE FOR THE ENTIRE SAMPLE

Figure 14. Color use by hospitals.

77

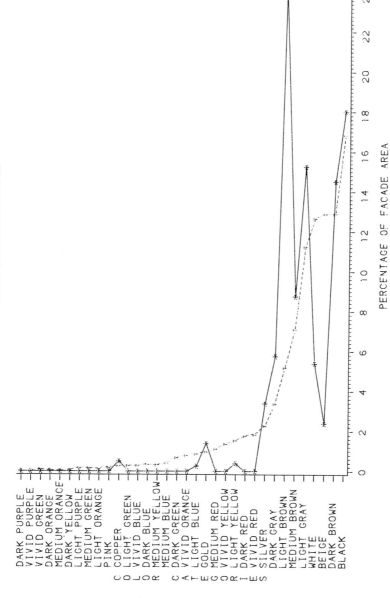

Figure 15. Color use by funeral homes.

78

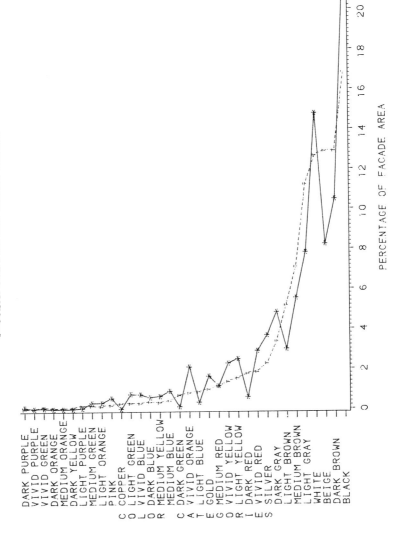

PERCENTAGE OF FACADE AREA

Figure 16. Color use by retail establishments.

similarities, statistically significant differences among the three groups emerged. Churches, banks, public institutions, and funeral homes, were confirmed in their use of color schemes quite different from those of hospitals, educational institutions, and hotels as a group, and different also from those of restaurants and shops taken together. Color use on the facades of hospitals, educational institutions, and hotels, in turn, was distinctively different from that of restaurants and shops.

TABLE 4

COLOR USE BY BANKS, CHURCHES, PUBLIC INSTITUTIONS, AND FUNERAL HOMES

Source	df	SS	F value	Pr > F
1. Number of Color Categories				
Model	3	4.11	0.62	0.73
Error	111	246.42		
Total	114	250.53		
2. Percentage of Facade Devoted to the Color Categories				
Model	3	15.09	0.04	0.98
Error	1220	165920.00		
Total	1223	165935.09		

TABLE 5

COLOR USE BY HOTELS, EDUCATIONAL INSTITUTIONS, AND HOSPITALS

Source	df	SS	F value	Pr > F
1. Number of Color Categories				
Model	2	2.07	0.48	0.62
Error	144	311.52		
Total	146	313.59		
2. Percentage of Facade Devoted to the Color Categories				
Model	2	11.61	0.05	0.95
Error	1860	233206.80		
Total	1862	233218.41		

With these points established, it appeared to be worth considering whether subtle differences in the function of organizations or in their clienteles might be related to color schemes. Six possible relationships were examined.

First, color schemes of banks were compared to those of savings-and-loan associations. Although these two types of organization differ somewhat in function and attempt to attract slightly different clienteles, no significant difference was found either in the number of colors they used or in the proportion of facade devoted to each color (table 7, figures 7 and 8).

TABLE 6

COLOR USE BY RESTAURANTS AND RETAIL ESTABLISHMENTS

Source	df	SS	F value	Pr > F
1. Number of Color Categories				
Model	1	1.50	0.63	0.85
Error	220	520.23		
Total	221	521.73		
2. Percentage of Facade Devoted to the Color Categories				
Model	1	5.71	0.04	0.98
Error	3200	451936.00		
Total	3201	451941.71		

TABLE 7

COLOR USE BY BANKS AND SAVINGS-AND-LOAN ASSOCIATIONS

Source	df	SS	F value	Pr > F
1. Number of Color Categories				
Model	1	6.97	3.69	0.06
Error	47	88.67		
Total	48	95.64		
2. Percentage of Facade Devoted to the Color Categories				
Model	1	4.78	0.05	0.99
Error	1223	164694.44		
Total	1224	164699.22		

Second, the relationship between color use and cuisine was investigated on the basis of data gathered from Chinese, Japanese, Greek, Italian, Mexican, French, Soul-food, and Sea-food restaurants, as well as steakhouses. These restaurants displayed significant differences in the use of color (table 8). By regrouping them it was discovered that, generally speaking, Chinese, Mexican, and Greek restaurants differed most noticeably from the others. Chinese restaurants used more vivid red and vivid yellow, Mexican restaurants used more white and vivid red, while Greek restaurants used more light blue and vivid blue.[1]

Third, the relationship between color use and religious denomination was examined. The denominations surveyed included Roman Catholic, Greek Orthodox, United Methodist, Lutheran (ALC), Presbyterian, Baptist (American), Christian Science, and Jewish, as well as a collection of unaffiliated churches, virtually all of the storefront type. Analysis revealed no

1. These and subsequent color names are technical terms referring to the color categories defined in chapter III.

TABLE 8

COLOR USE AND RESTAURANT CUISINE

Source	df	SS	F value	Pr > F
1. Number of Color Categories				
Model	8	227.18	6.73	<.001
Error	75	316.63		
Total	83	543.81		
2. Percentage of Facade Devoted to the Color Categories				
Model	8	5025.38	7.33	<.001
Error	1031	88297.82		
Total	1039	93323.20		

significant differences in color use (table 9), all denominations used few and neutral colors over large proportions of their facades. Storefront churches, it is true, exhibited somewhat more chromatically variegated facades, being especially partial to vivid shades of red, yellow, and green, but this difference was insignificant statistically. The only other noteworthy feature of the facades of religious organizations was their use of metal. Although the fact will be discussed subsequently, it should be remarked here that the facades of places of worship stand apart from all others in their use of copper. The soft, green patina of this metal, common on churches, was rarely observed anywhere else.

TABLE 9

COLOR USE AND RELIGIOUS DENOMINATION

Source	df	SS	F value	Pr > F
1. Number of Color Categories				
Model	8	18.41	0.96	0.48
Error	57	136.82		
Total	65	155.17		
2. Percentage of Facade Devoted to the Color Categories				
Model	8	114.76	0.86	0.56
Error	1080	18074.32		
Total	1088	118935.82		

Fourth, a sample of men's and women's clothing stores was analysed for any relationship that might exist between color use and differentiation within a particular type of organization. So that color use strictly according to gender-defined clientele could be studied, stores offering both men's and women's clothes were excluded. Moreover, because a relationship between color use and price range was known to exist (see later discussion), the samples of men's and women's stores were matched as to price level. Table

10 shows that results of the analysis were mixed. Although there was a difference in the colors used by these two types of shop, manifested chiefly in the more frequent occurence of light gray, light yellow, vivid orange, and vivid red among women's clothiers (figures 17 and 18), the proportion of facade area devoted to these colors did not differ significantly.

TABLE 10

COLOR USE BY MEN'S AND WOMEN'S CLOTHING STORES

Source	df	SS	F value	Pr > F
1. Number of Color Categories				
Model	1	40.45	8.18	0.006
Error	75	370.78		
Total	76	411.23		
2. Percentage of Facade Devoted to the Color Categories				
Model	1	9.07	2.43	0.15
Error	1500	5598.77		
Total	1501	5607.84		

Fifth, hotels and motels (or motor inns) were compared, as types of organization offering very similar services but seeking slightly different clienteles. Again, the samples were matched as to price. It was discovered that motels tend to use a greater number of colors than do hotels, and to cover a greater proportion of their facades with vivid colors or colors principally drawn from the red, yellow, green, and blue hues (table 11, figures 9 and 19).

TABLE 11

COLOR USE BY HOTELS AND MOTELS

Source	df	SS	F value	Pr > F
1. Number of Color Categories				
Model	1	20.73	7.17	.012
Error	98	283.15		
Total	99	303.88		
2. Percentage of Facade Devoted to the Color Categories				
Model	1	60.23	6.98	.001
Error	600	5177.36		
Total	601	5237.59		

Sixth, hotels were compared with one another, having been grouped into three categories: convention hotels, residential and transient hotels, and businessmen's and tourist hotels. Analysis revealed no significant difference in color use among the categories (table 12). Each group used essentially the same number of colors, and apportioned them in much the same manner on facades.

83

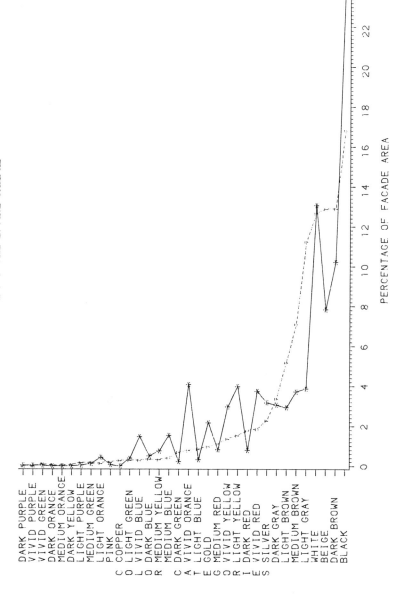

Figure 17. Color use by men's clothing stores.

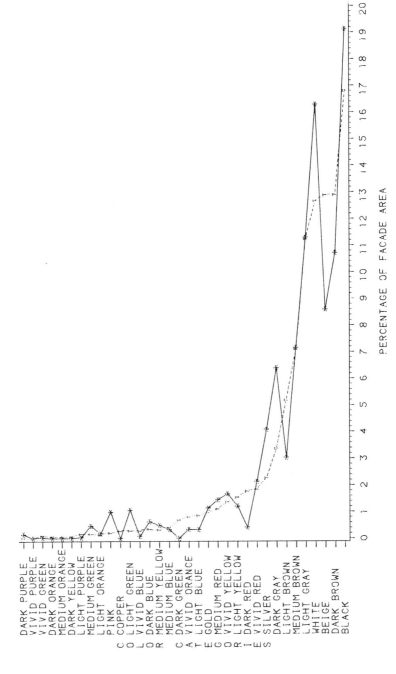

Figure 18 Color use by women's clothing stores.

85

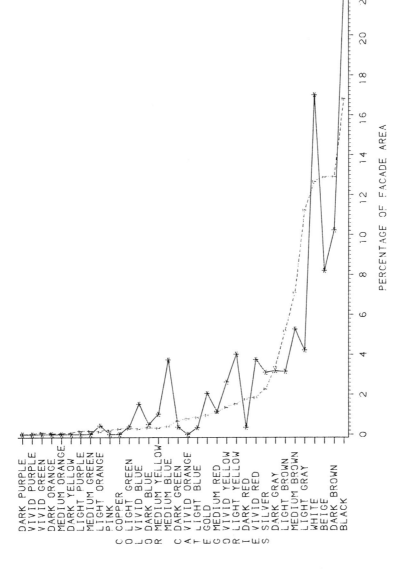

*=COLOR USE BY MOTELS
T=COLOR USE FOR THE ENTIRE SAMPLE

Figure 19. Color use by motels.

TABLE 12

COLOR USE AND HOTELS, BY CLIENTELE

Source	df	SS	F value	Pr > F
1. Number of Color Categories				
Model	2	29.46	3.65	0.03
Error	79	319.03		
Total	81	348.49		
2. Percentage of Facade Devoted to the Color Categories				
Model	2	8.37	1.16	0.31
Error	621	2240.42		
Total	623	2248.79		

These six analyses, half of them revealing a statistically significant relation between institutional activity and color use and the other half not doing so, point toward difficult problems of explanation, and hence serve as something of a special introduction to the concerns of chapter V.

Price Level and Color Use

Field observation suggested that the price level of goods and services offered by organizations might bear a significant relation to color use. It seemed that, as price increased, fewer colors were used on facades and that they tended more toward the achromatic or monochromatic-brown ranges. This hypothesis was tested for restaurants, hotels, and clothing stores.

Price levels for restaurants in the sample were relatively easily determined. By cross-checking menus and price lists against various restaurant guides, it was possible to derive an average-price statistic for each establishment. This figure was calculated in one of two ways. If a restaurant offered complete meals the prices of the dinners were averaged. Where menus were specified on a price-per-item basis (as in most cafeterias and fast food restaurants) a representative meal, including a beverage, was priced.[2] The sample was divided into four categories: those greater than one standard deviation above the mean ($18.15 and above); those between the mean and one standard deviation above the mean (from $12.07 to $18.14); those between the mean and one standard deviation below (from $5.99 to $12.06); and those greater than one standard deviation below the mean (less than $5.99).

2. The average price of a meal at the restaurants in this sample was $12.07 (s.d. 6.08).

The category with lowest prices comprised mostly fast-food shops, cafeterias, delicatessens, and hot dog stands. There might or might not have been room for sit-down dining. The next higher category included restaurants providing service to seated customers, generally office workers, business people, and others attracted by the proximity of these establishments to their place of work. These were not generally restaurants to which people would plan a special visit. In contrast, restaurants from the third category tended to be of a set which, with or without a city-wide reputation, could draw customers from a distance by virtue of menu, service, or ambiance. Establishments in this category were often patronized by visitors and tourists and were likely to advertise. (Fast-food restaurants also advertise but on a chain rather than on a restaurant by restaurant basis). Restaurants of the fourth and highest-priced category generally were of a celebrated sort, known to be costly, and thought to be suitable as venues for special occasions. They were drawn from the group that appears in guides to the city's best restaurants, and that may be expected to insist on a certain formality of dress and etiquette.[3]

Table 13 shows that restaurants were, in fact, differentiated by color in the way that had been suspected during the field survey: the more expensive the restaurant, the fewer colors on its facade, and the more extensive the use of achromatic-neutral and monochromatic-brown tones. The lowest-priced restaurants tended to be set apart by the use of vivid colors. The color composition of the facades assigned to the four categories can be studied in figures 20, 21, 22, and 23.

TABLE 13

COLOR USE AND THE PRICE LEVEL OF RESTAURANTS

Source	df	SS	F value	Pr > F
1. Number of Color Categories				
Model	3	439.18	29.73	.001
Error	187	920.80		
Total	190	1359.97		
2. Percentage of Facade Devoted to the Color Categories				
Model	51	64363.92	20.59	.001
Error	2431	148983.97		
Total	2482	213347.89		

3. This categorization of restaurants is, interestingly, reflected in the variety and range of beverages offered. Generally speaking only non-alcoholic drinks are available in restaurants of the first category. Liquor is served in restaurants of the next higher type but the selection is limited. Restaurants of the third category include among their offerings a limited wine list, while restaurants of the final category offer all the beverages mentioned thus far, supplemented by an expanded wine list.

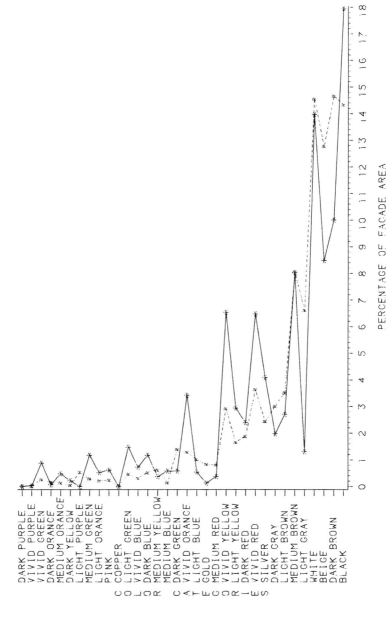

Figure 20. Color use by restaurants priced to $5.98.

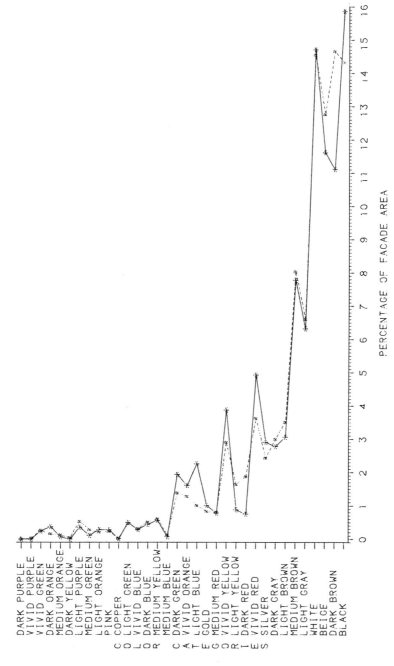

*=COLOR USE BY RESTAURANTS PRICED $5.99-$12.06
R=COLOR USE FOR ALL RESTAURANTS

Figure 21. Color use by restaurants priced $5.99-$12.06.

90

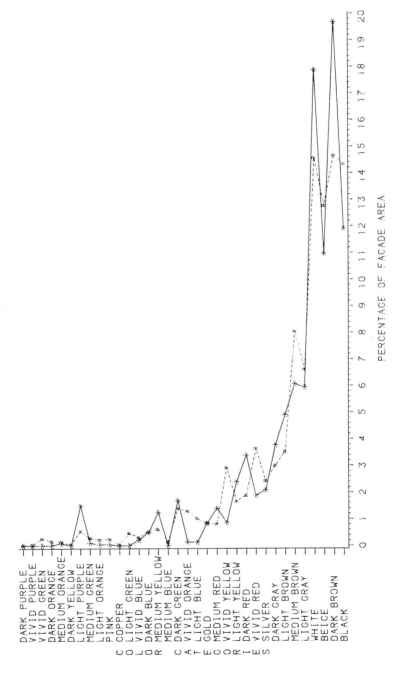

Figure 22. Color use by restaurants priced $12.07–$18.14

91

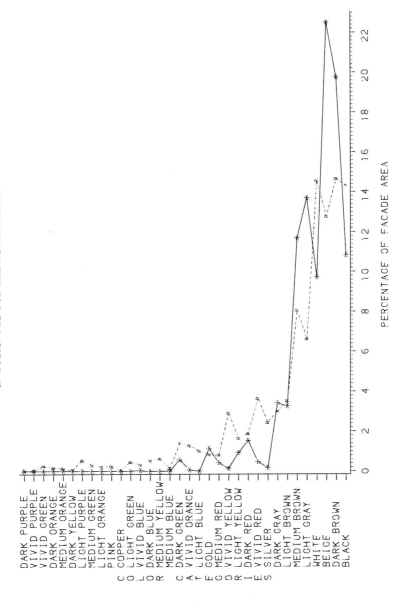

Figure 23. Color use by restaurants priced $18.15 and above.

A similar type of analysis was applied to hotels, the price
level in this instance having been established on the basis of the
daily rate for the least expensive single room.[4] Categories were
defined, as in the case of restaurants, by standard deviations above
and below the mean. The ranges were: less than $13.07;
$13.07-$39.27; $39.28-$65.48; $65.49-$91.70; and greater than
$91.70. As table 14 shows, there was no statistically significant
relationship between the price level of hotels and the use of color.

TABLE 14

COLOR USE AND THE PRICE LEVEL OF HOTELS

Source	df	SS	F value	Pr > F
1. Number of Color Categories				
Model	4	23.60	1.40	0.24
Error	77	324.89		
Total	81	348.49		
2. Percentage of Facade Devoted to the Color Categories				
Model	4	9.88	1.16	0.33
Error	1640	3493.20		
Total	1645	3503.08		

The relation of price range to color use was also analyzed
for a sample of both men's and women's retail clothing stores.
Initially an attempt was made to establish the price levels of these
shops by pricing a broad range of goods at each shop. However, this
proved impossible owing to differences in the quality and range of
goods offered in the sample shops and because in many cases clerks
were uncooperative. As a practical expedient, price levels were
determined only for a restricted set of goods, with the result that
three categories were designated: (1) discount stores and factory
and warehouse outlets; (2) shops pricing some goods as low as
those found in discount houses but also offering items at
noticeably higher prices (e.g $20-$50 for a shirt, blouse, or
pair of trousers or perhaps $150-$300 for a suit); (3) shops, such
as designer boutiques and clothiers with national or even
international reputations, selling merchandise almost exclusively at
the higher limits of a product's price range.

In the belief that this classification corresponded
sufficiently with gross differences in the price of goods offered
for sale, the risk was taken of identifying the categories of
clothing shop as "least expensive," "intermediate," and "most

---

4. The average price of a room for the hotels in this sample was $39.28
(s.d. 26.21).

expensive." Table 15 reveals statistically significant differences in color use by clothing stores of the three classes. Generally speaking, stores in the most expensive category used the fewest colors on their facades, and the fewest vivid hues. Those in the least expensive category used the largest number of colors, emphasizing vivid hues of red and yellow. Shops of the intermediate category tended to use color schemes between these two extremes. The details of these color compositions are displayed in figures 24, 25, 26.

TABLE 15

COLOR USE AND THE PRICE LEVEL OF CLOTHING SHOPS

Source	df	SS	F value	Pr > F
	1. Number of Color Categories			
Model	2	98.31	8.31	.001
Error	74	437.11		
Total	76	535.42		
	2. Percentage of Facade Devoted to the Color Categories			
Model	2	18.21	7.17	.001
Error	1891	2392.64		
Total	1893	2410.85		

The results of these three analyses are mixed, indicating a strong relation between color of facade and price for restaurant and clothing stores, but no relation at all for hotels. The inference once again is that although color plays an important part in some interactions, caution is advisable in anticipating the degree of its involvement.

Organizational Size and Color Use

In keeping with the broadly exploratory nature of the present study, it would have been desirable to test for relations between organizational size and facade color, across all types of organization. However, many impediments arose. Sometimes, needed statistics could not be obtained. Shop owners and managers were often reluctant to disclose either volume of sales or number of customers. Not all religious organizations were willing to divulge either size of membership or size of budget. Sometimes, although the desired information was forthcoming, there were too few organizations of a particular type to provide an adequate sample. This was true, for example, of educational institutions, for which enrollment figures were available, and hospitals, from which numbers of beds could be obtained. Yet another difficulty was encountered in the case of public institutions: noncomparability among the

94

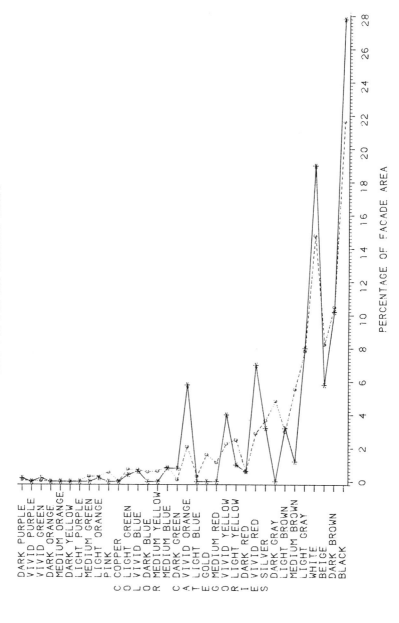

*=COLOR USE BY THE LEAST EXPENSIVE CLOTHING SHOPS
C=COLOR USE FOR ALL CLOTHING SHOPS

Figure 24. Color use by the least expensive clothing shops.

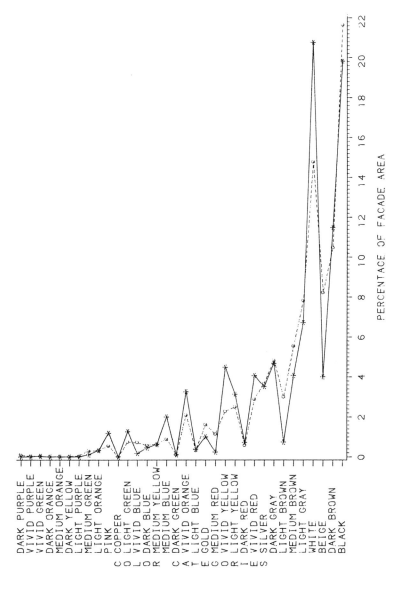

Figure 25. Color use by clothing shops of intermediate price.

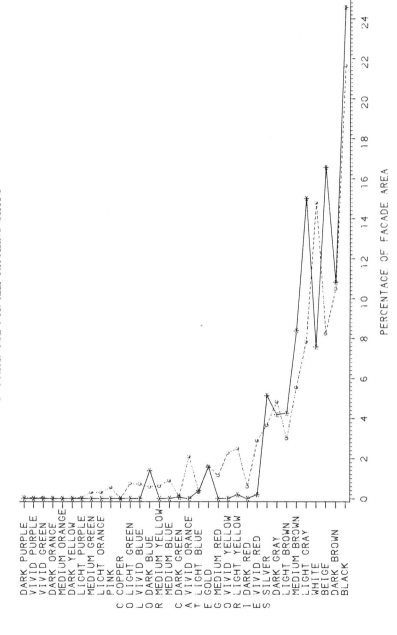

*=COLOR USE BY THE MOST EXPENSIVE CLOTHING SHOPS
C=COLOR USE FOR ALL CLOTHING SHOPS

Figure 26. Color use by the most expensive clothing shops.

sub-types (for instance, the size index appropriate to a court
system and that appropriate to a harbor control authority). After
elimination by these factors, only banks, hotels, and
savings-and-loan associations remained, as organizations amenable to
analysis.

The sizes of banks and savings-and-loan associations were
defined by the value of their total assets.[5] Four categories were
recognized on the basis of standard deviations above and below the
mean.[6] Analyses of the categories are presented in tables 16 and 17.
In both cases organizational size was found to be unrelated to color
use.

TABLE 16

COLOR USE AND BANK SIZE

Source	df	SS	F value	Pr > F
1. Number of Color Categories				
Model	3	9.06	1.57	0.22
Error	45	86.58		
Total	48	99.64		
2. Percentage of Facade Devoted to the Color Categories				
Model	3	15.54	0.98	0.38
Error	960	5074.29		
Total	963	5089.83		

For size of hotel, the total number of rooms was adopted as an
index.[7] Categories were again defined on the basis of standard
deviations from the sample mean:[8] fewer than 482 rooms; 482-997

---

5. The asset value of banks was obtained from Sherry McFall, ed., *Chicago
Banks: Directory of Officers and Financial Statements and Suburban Cook County
Bank Officers* (Chicago: Law Bulletin Publishing Co., January 1981).
The asset value of savings-and-loan associations was obtained from the
Chicago Savings-and-Loan Association Information Office.

6. The average value of assets controlled by Chicago area
savings-and-loan associations was $183,360,000 (s.d. 426,020,000). On the other
hand the calculation of the average size of banks by assets was skewed,
initially, by the disproportionate size of the eight largest banks, which were up
to a thousand times the size of the smallest. Because of this the mean and
standard deviation used in this study were computed by excluding these eight
banks (American National Bank and Trust, Continental Illinois Bank, Credit
Agricole, Credit Lyonnnais, First National Bank of Chicago, Harris Bank and
Trust, Lasalle National Bank, and Northern Trust Bank) from the calculation. The
average size of the remaining banks was $724,570,000 (s.d. 406,920,000). Some
of the banks that had been excluded from the calculation of average assets
were surveyed and included in the sample of facades. Of course, they were
placed in the highest category.

7. These figures were obtained from the hotels themselves. Most were also
listed in hotel and motel guides including American Automobile Association,
Tourbook: Illinois, Indiana, Ohio 1981 (Falls Church, Va.: American Automobile
Association, 1981); Illinois Hotel and Motel Association, *Illinois Hotel/Motel
Directory, 1981-1982* (Springfield: State of Illinois, The Office of Tourism,
Department of Commerce and Community Affairs, 1981); and Rand McNally and Co.,
Mobil Travel Guide: Great Lakes Area, 1981 (Chicago: Rand McNally and Co., 1981).

8. The average size of hotels in central Chicago was 482 rooms (s.d.
514.59).

TABLE 17

COLOR USE AND THE SIZE OF SAVINGS-AND-LOAN ASSOCIATIONS

Source	df	SS	F value	Pr > F
1. Number of Color Categories				
Model	3	8.94	1.82	0.18
Error	30	49.12		
Total	33	58.06		
2. Percentage of Facade Devoted to the Color Categories				
Model	3	1531.29	1.63	0.20
Error	600	1531.29		
Total	603	1543.77		

rooms; and more than 997 rooms. Analysis showed that there was no statistically significant relation between hotel size and color use (table 18).

TABLE 18

COLOR USE AND HOTEL SIZE

Source	df	SS	F value	Pr > F
1. Number of Color Categories				
Model	2	7.54	1.91	0.16
Error	60	118.43		
Total	62	125.97		
2. Percentage of Facade Devoted to the Color Categories				
Model	2	10.11	2.49	0.08
Error	1200	2436.14		
Total	1202	2446.25		

The the uniformly negative results of these few analyses suggest that organizational size in general bears no relation to color use on facades.

Organizational Age and Color Use

In mounting an analysis of organizational age[9] as it might relate to patterns of color use we were faced with much the same problems as those that beset the exploration of size and color. Educational institutions and hospitals again had to be excluded for lack of a sufficiently large sample size and public institutions because of their noncomparability. Religious organizations were

---

9. It is important to note that we are dealing here with the time elapsed since organizations were founded, not the ages of the buildings that organizations occupy. During its lifetime an organization may have occupied a series of buildings of different ages. As a separate matter, the age of a building may be expected to bear a significant relation to the process of communication, insofar as the date of construction is almost always associated with architectural style.

amenable to analysis but the skewed distribution of church ages in the sample prevented any analysis more sophisticated than that of old versus new churches. No special difficulties were encountered in analyzing the age-color relationship with respect to hotels, clothing stores, and banks.[10]

Analysis of organizational age for churches was based, as noted above, on a simple dichotomy between older (50 or more years old) and younger (less then 50 years old). The results of the analysis, presented in table 19, show no significant difference in the use of color by these two groups. In the analysis of clothing shops four categories were set up on the customary basis of mean and standard deviation.[11] The ranges of the categories were: older than 44 years; 30-44 years old; 16-29 years old; and less than 16 years old. There appeared to be no significant relation between the age of the organizations and their use of color (table 20). However the relation proved to be very slightly stronger than in the case with churches. Using the same procedures, four categories of bank were distinguished.[12] Once again no significant relation was found between age and use of color (table 21). In the analysis of hotels three categories were discriminated.[13] For the third time no statistically significant relationship was apparent between age of institution and use of color (table 22). These analyses almost compel a general conclusion for organizational age like that for organizational size: no bearing on color use.

TABLE 19

COLOR USE AND CHURCH AGE

Source	df	SS	F value	Pr > F
1. Number of Color Categories				
Model	1	4.73	0.78	0.38
Error	40	242.56		
Total	41	247.29		
2. Percentage of Facade Devoted to the Color Categories				
Model	1	7.25	2.13	0.16
Error	800	2723.00		
Total	801	2730.25		

10. It was not thought worthwhile to extend the exploration to savings-and-loan associations since banks and savings-and-loan associations had shown no difference in their use of color in other contexts.

11. The average age of clothing shops in this sample was 30 years (s.d. 14).

12. The average age of banks was 65 years (s.d. 22).

13. The average age of the hotels was 45 years (s.d. 19).

TABLE 20

COLOR USE AND THE AGE OF CLOTHING STORES

Source	df	SS	F value	Pr > F
1. Number of Color Categories				
Model	3	7.08	0.76	0.47
Error	121	375.74		
Total	124	382.82		
2. Percentage of Facade Devoted to the Color Categories				
Model	3	28.68	1.11	0.33
Error	2430	20928.65		
Total	2433	20957.33		

TABLE 21

COLOR USE AND BANK AGE

Source	df	SS	F value	Pr > F
1. Number of Color Categories				
Model	3	8.58	1.76	0.18
Error	45	73.13		
Total	48	81.71		
2. Percentage of Facade Devoted to the Color Categories				
Model	3	10.52	2.54	0.08
Error	900	1242.52		
Total	903	1253.04		

TABLE 22

COLOR USE AND HOTEL AGE

Source	df	SS	F value	Pr > F
1. Number of Color Categories				
Model	2	4.23	0.77	0.47
Error	54	148.32		
Total	56	152.55		
2. Percentage of Facade Devoted to the Color Categories				
Model	2	12.46	3.02	0.05
Error	1080	2227.95		
Total	1082	2240.41		

The Color Repertoire

An aspect of color use in public spaces which has not yet received direct comment is preference for specific colors--or choices from the total repertoire of colors--reflected in this study's sample of facades. To begin, color use was always skewed to include a disproportionate share of achromatic hues and monochromatic-brown hues (figures 7-26 inclusive). To achieve discrimination across the full range of the distribution each of the relationships studied in previous sections was re-analyzed, treating each color as a separate variable. The results are described below.

Color categories registering significant differences over all organizational types were (at the .01 level): white, light gray, black, vivid red, medium orange, light brown, vivid yellow, and medium blue. Vivid red, medium orange, vivid yellow, medium green, and light blue showed significant differences according to types of restaurant cuisine. The distinction between hotels and motels lay principally in the presence of vivid red, vivid orange, light yellow, and light blue on the facades of the latter, and the difference between men's and women's clothing stores was evident mainly in the use of vivid red, light red, vivid yellow, light yellow, light green, and medium orange by the latter. In the case of restaurants, differences in price level tended to be associated with a down-scale increase in the use of light gray, vivid red, vivid orange, vivid yellow, light green, and vivid green, whereas differences in the price level of hotels were likely to be differentiated by a downward increase in the use of white and vivid red. Organizational age and size were never associated with distinct patterns of color use.

Metals and Lights

Three metallic hues and six hues of light were measured during the process of photo-transcription and analyzed for each of the relations considered in this study. Although silver-hued metals (aluminum, steel, chromium, and silver) were never associated with any of the relations in which we are interested, the use of yellow and yellow-brown hued metals (bronze, brass, gold) and copper were almost invariably associated with organizations employing few colors and more "formal" color schemes. These hues predominated on civic buildings, banks, churches, expensive hotels, high-class restaurants, and exclusive shops. Copper was a virtual perogative of religious organizations. Lights (of any of the hues specified in chapter III) were used predominantly by the cheapest restaurants, hotels, shops. Their incidence on facades was found to parallel the utilization of vivid shades of the primary hues. Over all, metals and lights were distributed in a complementary fashion: organizations favoring yellow metals and copper tended to avoid colored lights, and vice versa.

Plants

Plants of many sorts figured prominently in the appearance of the sample facades. When plant coverage (which included trees planted in walkways) was transcribed from photos for its share of facade area independent of color (figure 27), two general findings resulted. First, exterior greenery was often associated with the organizations that used copper, the yellow-hued metals, and a small selection of colors nearly always drawn from the achromatic or monochromatic-brown ranges. This was especially true of the more exclusive hotels, restaurants, and clothing stores where the relative extent of plant coverage across the facade (as viewed by the camera) was directly related to price level. Second, while plant use was found to parallel color use as a whole in the major relations under study, the same was not true of its analog, the on-the-building color green, if only because the latter was not used as frequently as or in as large a quantity as many other hues. It sometimes seemed as if plants were being employed as substitutes for the color green on the exteriors of buildings.

Signs

The analysis also involved measurement of the proportion of facade area covered by signs (as before, independent of color). Sign use was found to be closely related to the use of metals, lights, and plants (figure 28). On the one hand, public institutions, banks, churches, savings-and-loan associations, and expensive hotels, restaurants, and shops tend to devote only a small proportion of their facades to signs, sometimes restricting them to street numbers or small brass nameplates. On the other hand, organizations using vivid colors and lights were likely to give over a large part of their facades to signs. In extreme cases (cheap restaurants for example), the entire facade constituted one large sign.

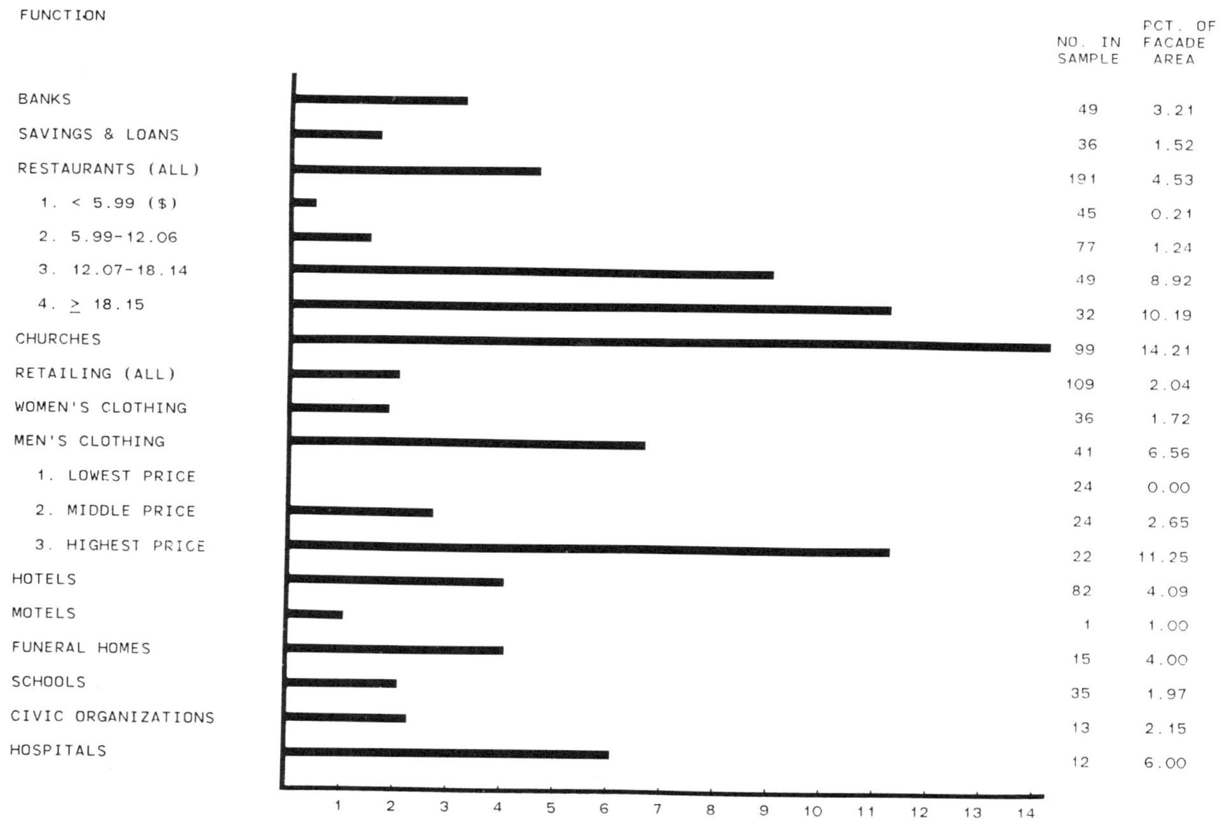

103

Figure 27. Plants and organizational type.

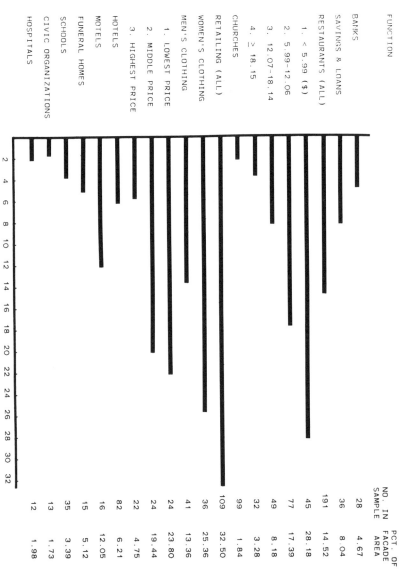

FUNCTION	NO. IN SAMPLE	PCT. OF FACADE AREA
BANKS	28	4.67
SAVINGS & LOANS	36	8.04
RESTAURANTS (ALL)	191	14.52
1. < 5.99 ($)	45	28.18
2. 5.99-12.06	77	17.39
3. 12.07-18.14	49	8.18
4. ≥ 18.15	32	3.28
CHURCHES	99	1.84
RETAILING (ALL)	109	32.50
WOMEN'S CLOTHING	36	25.36
MEN'S CLOTHING	41	13.36
1. LOWEST PRICE	24	23.80
2. MIDDLE PRICE	24	19.44
3. HIGHEST PRICE	22	4.75
HOTELS	82	6.21
MOTELS	16	12.05
FUNERAL HOMES	15	5.12
SCHOOLS	35	3.39
CIVIC ORGANIZATIONS	13	1.73
HOSPITALS	12	1.98

Figure 28. Signs and organizational type.

CHAPTER V

A COMMUNICATION-BASED INTERPRETATION OF THE RESULTS

The findings in chapter IV confirm that color is more than a merely incidental adjunct to social action yet something less than a key indicator of institutional role. The findings strongly suggest that essentially the same is true of other facets of material expression. If we disregard the words that almost always appear on building facades and consider only material expression, it turns out that if one facet, say color, provides no information about the organization behind the facade, another component or combination of components will. That is, aspects of material expression tend to complement one another. Whereas the size of a building is most often related to the size of the occupying organization, people on the street have to use such cues as color, siting, architectural style, or material composition to determine whether a structure of a given size houses a bank or a factory.

Moreover, if we enlarge the scope of our inquiry we discover that encounters in public spaces and the use of cues displayed on facades are not always essential to any given type of transaction. People can bank by mail, shop by catalogue over the telephone or, again, through the mail, or dine at home rather than in a restaurant. They are not forced always to enter public spaces in order to find suitable settings for exchange and interaction, and these alternative interactions may make use of quite different props and material objects. It seems true that, for all but the most ritualized of cultural interactions, there are always forms of social interaction which can substitute for or render superfluous any given interaction without disrupting the flow of social behavior.

These points provide background for the two questions which this chapter must address. First, why do we find that organizations of differing functional category, or those offering goods at varying price levels within a category, usually can be distinguished by the color schemes of their facades? Second, why do we sometimes find that organizations of very different function use virtually identical color schemes for their facades? Restated, why is it that generally speaking banks, restaurants, and shops use very different color schemes, while banks, high-priced restaurants, and high-priced shops share the same color scheme without seeming to confuse their patrons?

The Coloration of Facades: Choices Among Modes of Communication

The first question can be answered by considering the relation between the kind of interaction chosen for study and the context of organizational action within which it is found. This analysis has concentrated upon a single type of interaction, or linkage, involving individual behavior in public space. When this linkage is considered as it fits into the entire range of linkages the organizations participate in, a good deal of difference among the organizations in our sample population is revealed. The interaction we have studied is suspended in a web of other interactions. Within this web, its significance varies widely by organizational type.

When a person seeks to establish relations with a bank it is not enough to walk into the lobby. Forms must be signed, accounts must be opened or closed, and contracts must be negotiated. Any single transaction requires both the individual and the bank to continue their relationship in a series of interactions. Walking through the door and recognizing the bank as a separate entity bordering on a public space are interactions that may be defined and studied (as in the present investigation) but in the total scope of an individual's involvement with the bank such interactions can be almost inconsequential. The same is true of encounters with religious organizations and governmental institutions. In order for an individual to make effective use of church or governmental power, relations must be sustained over long periods of time and will include many interactions having little or nothing to do with any single visit an individual might have paid to an organization's headquarters.

The situation is different for restaurants and shops. The interaction introduced by a person standing before the facade of a shop deciding whether or not to enter one of these establishments constitutes a critical juncture in the relationship between these organizations and the individual. Once an individual has decided to enter a shop, has selected some article for purchase, has paid for it, and has departed from the store, the set of necessary interactions is closed. The individual need never engage in another interaction with that particular retailer for this one interaction to succeed. The same is true of restaurants, especially those of low price. The facade is an attraction, a means of marketing, which will be important to success or failure. The interactions that occur inside a restaurant may be more directly related to this success or failure, but interaction at the facade will, generally speaking, play a far larger part in the operation of low-priced restaurants than in the functioning of a bank or church.

To generalize, the differing goals of organizations are likely to place different demands upon their facades. Those organizations which see the facade as an essential contribution to their success will be inclined to draw attention to themselves by the use of bright colors, or unusual combinations and patterns of color--at least as long as their color scheme does not misrepresent their interests in some way. There are definite limits to the patterns from which they can choose; an inappropriate or misrepresentative facade may actually impair the interactions which they are trying to promote.

Although organizations such as banks and churches whose viability depends upon continued interaction with the same individuals over prolonged periods of time have an incentive to announce themselves appropriately in public spaces, it is not necessary that their facades draw attention in quite the same way as must those of shops and restaurants. Only a small number of people are likely to make their first contact with a bank, church, or government institution as the result of an unpremeditated encounter with a facade overlooking a public space. Most select their bank or church on the basis of knowledge acquired in previous interactions. Other than marking their presence in some way, the facades of such organizations can maintain a certain neutrality.

Some organizations are faced with the problem of framing, by facade, two or more dissimilar modes of public interaction. Hospitals are a case in point. On the one hand their provision of emergency care requires them to mark their emergency rooms so that ready access at street level is assured. Consequently, emergency entrances are brightly colored and well-lit; they contrast with their surroundings. On the other hand, hospitals also provide longer-term care, which normally requires patients to engage in a series of interactions with hospital staff. The walk through the door of the hospital is perhaps the least of these interactions. It follows that a hospital is justified in maintaining, for the most part, a certain chromatic neutrality at street level.

Thus far we have drawn some general conclusions on coloration of facades in relation to the frequency and duration of interactions between an organization and its clients. During the process of photo-transcription, it was possible not only to record color use, but also to measure the proportion of facade given over to exterior signs and posters. As was noted in chapter IV, this proportion was found to be statistically associated with the same relationships as was color. We learned that banks, churches, and public institutions as a class devoted a smaller percentage of their facades to signs than did shops and restaurants. Those organizations which depend upon their facades to draw people into short-term interactions (as do restaurants and shops) find it advantageous to display more and larger signs. It is not just a question of the sign's catching the attention of passersby, but also of its serving as a ready source of information. Signs give the passing individual an idea of what goes on behind the facade and of the obligations the individual might expect to assume upon going inside. Such organizations do not require that individuals establish long-term relationships with them. A customer's first and last contact may be practically at the front door.

Banks, churches, public institutions, and other high-status organizations which seek to cultivate long-term interactions are little interested in establishing this sort of relation. A person may be drawn to a church by its ministry or to a bank by its reputation, without any involvement of the facade. For such an organization signs are less important for effective interaction than is its network of contacts with society as a whole. When it comes time to choose a facade, to put on a social costume so to speak, these organizations can establish their identity in public space with little more than a modest sign. They may prefer to remain almost anonymous at street level. If a facade is too flamboyant, if it attracts too much attention, it may draw the sort of individual inside who will not desire, or have the resources required, to establish the long-term chain of interactions upon which this type of organization depends. The signs they employ are often only inconspicuous brass nameplates bearing a name and street number.

Not only do these remarks on the use of signs support the development of our general objective--to understand the coloration of facades in the context of organizational interaction--but they also point toward the desirability of further enlarging the scope of discussion. It must be remembered that the on-the-street communicational resources available to an organization do not stop with signs and color. After all, if attention is what an organization is interested in attracting there are other means which may be equally or more effective. For example, barkers could be hired to stand outside restaurant doors to assail passersby with information. In fact, this occurs in places such as Bourbon Street in New Orleans where bright lights and vivid colors do not provide enough of a competitive advantage to taverns and saloons. If we were to give the problem of attention-getting some thought, as advertising agents are paid to do, we could devise many substitutes for or supplements to color on the facade. Regardless of the activities of an organization, it is presented with a choice as to how its goals are to be accomplished communicationally. It can use any channel (visual and aural being favorites) and any type of object or action available in its repertoire.

Optionality in Linkages

Energy transmitted by one channel during communication can be substituted for energy transmitted by another channel. Further, modes of communication within any given channel may be substituted one for another as well as for modes in other channels. Within limits any combination of channel and mode can be used to frame particular, significant features of interaction. Participants have a choice, subject to convention, and the choice they make is a source of information to other participants. A question that remains to be answered, given these options, is why do people choose to use material objects in some settings and not in others? With so many alternatives available, why do people use objects at all when it is possible, theoretically, to function without them?

The Option of Material Expression

The chief virtue of material expression (i.e. the use of props) is that, in comparison with energy transmitted through verbal and non-verbal behavior, it is long-lasting and transmits or reflects energy relatively permanently. Once props are created and deployed, special effort is required to remove them from the environment. This durability of physical objects largely determines their contribution to the communication process. Four specifications of contribution can be made (expanding upon four advantages of material expression presented in chapter II).

First, if certain types of information have to be transmitted over and over again it makes sense to use material objects to frame these interactions so that repetition of verbal and non-verbal behavior can be kept to a minimum.

Second, material objects can stand in for participants. The objects become agents, personal or impersonal, for the participant. In large part this is true of the facades studied in this project: they are agents during the initial contact between the organization and the individual. As go-betweens, they save a certain amount of effort (discounting the creation of the facade as a one-time capital investment) for both the organization and for the passerby. The organizations do not have to stand, so to speak, on the street and announce themselves. The person in the public space can make an evaluation quickly, making a decision on the basis of impersonal cues without having to engage in verbal or non-verbal exchange.

Third, some types of information which may be important to the interaction may be difficult to represent by other communicational means. For example, whereas sociolinguistic markers are reasonably effective indicators of class or social-group affiliation, they are less servicable as indices of power, authority, and hegemony. For these qualities material expression is often a more effective alternative. With prolonged use physical forms can be established as metaphors expressive of subjective concepts. Having become accustomed to a metaphor (such as physical size for status) people are no longer aware of the relationship that gave rise to it in the first place; status is size, and size is status. The interchangeability of one for the other has become spontaneous.[1]

Fourth, once established in an interaction, a material form can act as a backdrop for subsequent interactions, whether or not participants in these later interactions were the creators of the form. Special effort is required to destroy physical form. Thus the design of a business office can impose its own patterns of bureaucratic organization over a long term. As we appraise the built environment from this point of view, we soon discover that it is difficult to assign any particular material form to a single interaction. The interaction which gave rise to a form in the first place may have been terminated or abandoned long ago. A comprehensive understanding of agglomerations of material forms would be dependent upon a diachronic appraisal of interaction structure.

These four specifications go far toward clarifying the role of material objects in communication. Whenever people find a material object useful for any of these reasons. they are free to use it (although they are never obligated to do so). Moreover, identification of these four advantages helps one toward an understanding of material expressions very far removed from those studied in this project. The use of writing, for example, can be seen as an attempt to extend the life-span of verbal behavior into situations where repetition in the original form would either be

---

1. It is also true that, as concerns material forms, the creation of a large edifice, the use of expensive and rare materials, or the commissioning of a grand architectural design are all evidence that the responsible organization has succeeded in previous interactions and has exerted power, authority, or control. It is not just a matter of convenience that these physical forms come to represent these qualities. They are good markers since they are directly related to the structure and outcomes of many previous interactions.

time consuming (as with warning or informational signs) or otherwise impossible (as in a book by an author long since dead). Again, personal apparel can be regarded as a means of obviating the need endlessly to repeat declarations of social role and status. It is not necessary to repeat a message (such as "I am a mechanic,...judge, ...custodian") when clothing serves to inform us of that fact.

Material Expression in the Sample

The organizations in the sample, in employing material expression, can be seen to have exploited all four of the advantages described above. Yet, in keeping with the differing activity patterns of the organizations, they availed themselves of material expression in general and of color in particular, in very different ways. Each type of facade was suspended in a different context.

The Coloration of Facades: Choices Among Facets of Material Expression

The preceding discussion has responded to only the first of the two questions posed at the beginning of this chapter. The second question is now to be addressed: why do organizations performing very different roles, notably banks, civic buildings, high-priced restaurants, and high-priced shops, present virtually identical color schemes on their facades without risk of confusing their clientele? Conversely, why is it that organizations performing the same or similar roles sometimes present quite different color schemes without provoking confusion? Even now, when we have arrived at a knowledge of the principles that lead organizations to use material expression to their advantage, we still have not explained why people are not generally misled by some of the choices that organizations make.

Optionality in Facets of Material Expression

Patterns of color use must be evaluated in the light of the fact that color is only one facet of material expression.[2] Just as we recognized that linkages represent options for communicative expression, their significance having to be weighed against the overall span of an organization's activity, so we must see that the facets of material expression offer choices in particular interaction contexts. To understand why a particular linkage is selected we conceived of verbal and gestural behavior, and the use of material objects (material expression), as complementary

---

2. Material expression has many facets including color, size, material composition (construction materials in the case of buildings), architectural style, and such other characteristics as shape and spatial arrangement.

expenditures of energy. To understand why a particular facet of
material expression is chosen we must take into account the
complementarity of the many facets of material expression.

Properties of the Facets of Material Expression

There are so many aspects of social interaction that no one
facet of material expression has the capability of meeting the
demands of them all. If such a single facet as color were adequate
to this task, all of the components of an organization's identity
could be color-coded into the cityscape. In the absence of this
possibility people are obliged to make choices, differentiating
among and combining the many facets available to them. To
understand the principles underlying the choices they make we must
discriminate between the facilitating and impeding attributes of the
several facets.

Perhaps these principles can be discussed most effectively by
borrowing a hierarchy of terms from statistics--nominal, ordinal,
interval, and ratio. Nominal measurement is a categorization of a
variable's values into mutually exclusive and exhaustive subclasses.
Ordinal measurement not only classifies values but also ranks them
from high to low or from most to least. Interval measurement not
only classifies and ranks the values of variables but places them
along an equally spaced continuum. Ratio measurement completes the
hierarchy by adding an absolute and non-arbitrary zero point to
interval measurement.

Some facets of material expression such as height, width,
depth, and volume are measurable at the ratio level. Others, such
architectural style and building material, can be evaluated only at
the nominal level. As to color, although it is a function of the
perception of visible light, which is a ratio-level variable, its
representation in the Munsell system of notation is less readily
characterized. There, it is related not only to Hue, which is
indeed directly connected with the ratio-level spectrum of visible
light, but also to Value and Chroma, that is the "whiteness" or
"blackness" of a color and its saturation with respect to a neutral
gray scale. Accordingly, the perception of color takes on the
characteristics of an interval level variable, involving the ranking
of colors at equally spaced intervals unrelated to a fixed,
non-arbitrary zero point.

At this point, the difficulties faced by people choosing among
facets of material expression begin to become apparent. The
difficulty, for example, of using a ratio-level physical variable
such as volume to mark a nominal-level social variable such as
economic function is evident enough. The height, width, depth, or

volume of a building, taken alone, cannot be depended upon to tell people that the building houses a clothing shop rather than a bank. It is not surprising, therefore, that many facets of material expression are typically called into play together to spell out the social identity of an organization. It must be added that even a combination of facets may not be adequate, but at least it can be said that the limitations of any individual facet--which will vary in significance according to the dimension of social identity that is to be expressed--can be alleviated through the use of one or more other facets as communicative complements.

The Special Case of Color

The recognition of limits in no way denies that a particular facet of material expression may possess properties which render it especially appropriate for some communicational purposes. There are two properties of color, for instance, which often serve to make it an effective mediator of interaction.

First, color is easily perceived. Second, it is an efficient means of classification, especially in situations where quick identification and evaluation of alternatives is required for effective interaction. In our culture, movement and action in public spaces requires that decisions be made rapidly, in the amount of time it takes to walk or drive past a facade. In this type of situation color serves well as an initial grouping principle. The colors of shop facades can be different from those of financial establishments, and the colors of restaurant facades different from those of hotels, so that the person on the street need only attend to certain broad chromatic patterns. Such patterns are likely to be recognized more quickly than a sign can be read and to provide as much essential information as the sign itself.

Combining these two properties of color--ease of perception and classificatory efficiency--we can appreciate why color serves readily to alert participants to key facts of interaction structure. It is capable of indicating, in a sort of shorthand, the principal features of specific interactions: it carries a certain interactional valence, the power to evoke the constellation of experiences that will be required for successful negotiation, exchange, and interaction. In the terminology of the theory of human communication, the effectiveness of color resides in its power as a repertorial cue, its ability to signal the broad outlines of context and experience that are to be drawn into interaction.

Unlike other facets of material expression, the color repertoire remains relatively constant even in the face of dramatic changes in scale from interaction to interaction. Although color is

necessarily present wherever physical objects figure in
interactions, its perception always relates to a stable array of
color values regardless of whether it appears on a skyscraper or a
candy wrapper. The case is much different for other facets of
material expression. Material composition, for example, varies
widely with context, manifesting extreme changes in the array (or
"scale") of values whose recognition is required for effective
interaction. In public space, people are asked to distinguish among
many grades of stone, brick, wood, concrete, metal, and plastic. In
face-to-face interaction, people are asked to distinguish among
fabrics, leathers, metals, jewels, furs, plastics, and other
materials of sartorial adornment. Depending upon the context, the
physical size of props can vary from cubic microns to cubic miles.
The number of sounds that people are called upon to assess in spoken
communication can amount to billions. The inclusion in any
particular interaction of other than a small set drawn from these
great ranges is rare, so that in the course of usual interactions
there are pronounced discontinuities in their use. A complex system
of conventions is needed for the interpretation of any and all of
these aspects of human action.

The cultural conventions defining color use, by contrast, are
generally simpler, and the repertorial categories fewer in number.
It is true, admittedly, that very considerable intricacy can arise
in certain contexts. Subtle gradations of a single hue may frame
major socio-cultural differences. This seems to be the case, for
example, with regard to many ritual gatherings of both public and
private nature, including college graduations, festivals, fairs,
religious observances, and ceremonies of state. Even so, the
experience of color can almost always be evaluated against a common
and familiar chromatic scale. Even if a series of interactions
involves only a small section of the total scale, discontinuities in
color patterning are not so conspicuous as in other facets of
material expression. Finally, because color is present in just
about all interactions, participants have learned to interpret it in
routine ways.

Color in the Sample

It is now practicable to consider the special role of color in
public space. Analysis has already allowed us to express this
function in terms of three categories of color use. First, there
are organizations which were found to use few colors, and those
chiefly in the achromatic (white to black) or monochromatic-brown
ranges. If other hues were used, they were usually light shades of
the primary hues (generally in descending order of frequency,

yellow, red, blue, and green) or as small patches of the most vivid shades of these hues. The organizations best represented in this category were banks, savings-and-loan associations, churches, educational and civic institutions, funeral homes, high-priced restaurants, expensive hotels, and exclusive shops.

Second, there are those organizations which were found to introduce a great deal of vivid color into facade patterns predominantly given over to achromatic or monochromatic-brown hues. This group included low-priced or fast-food restaurants, the cheapest hotels, retail establishments in general, but more particularly those of the lowest price-range (discount houses, or stores during sales), theaters, garages, and filling stations.

Third, there were those organizations whose color schemes fell between these two extremes, including moderately priced restaurants, hotels, and retail establishments. These groups relied mainly on achromatic and monochromatic-brown hues, while excluding themselves from the second category by restricting vivid hues to smaller areas.

If these three groups were arrayed along a single axis, the termini could be variously labeled: high status/low status, sacred/secular, expensive/cheap, authority/lack of authority, control/lack of control. The greater the authority or status of an organization the more likely it will be to use a facade with few colors, and colors drawn from the neutral hues. The weaker the authority and the lower the status of an organization the brighter will be its color scheme. In view of the emphasis placed on money in our culture as a measure of status and authority, it is not surprising to find that the price level of restaurants or retail establishments is reflected in the color schemes of their facades. Moreover, churches, as institutions representing moral authority, generally contrast in color use with drinking establishments and other enterprises typically thought to oppose religious values.

These correspondences do not mean that color symbolizes status and authority. Rather, color plays its part in framing social interaction. Behavior in banks, churches, and prestigious restaurants is more restricted and formalized than behavior associated with organizations of lower status and authority. The color scheme is a cue to the range of behavior appropriate to a setting.

Color, as an orientation to interaction, can be associated with any variable that is important to the communication process. In our culture, proper orientation generally requires that we have information about the status and power of the organizations (and individuals) with whom we come into contact. But that does not mean that only organizations of high status and power will be allowed to use a given scheme. Whenever an organization (perhaps of low status) needs or wishes to establish a different-from-normal interaction with its audience, one which requires a more formal behavior, it can assume a different color scheme. Hence in times past upon the death of a family member the house truly became a "funeral home" with the addition of black to the facade. As a counter-example, when a high-status organization is reduced in condition it will often adopt a new costume of color. A going-out-of-business sale, signalling the collapse of an organization, is generally bannered with brightly colored signs.

It is not to be expected then that organizations of a given class will invariably be found to use the same color scheme. The scheme marks an orientation to interaction, and since the intended interaction varies even within a single status group, the marker will vary accordingly.

Additional Aspects of Optionality in the Sample

In the sample, choice involving all of the properties of color previously listed, as well as the various manifestations of optionality relating color to other facets (in acts of substitution, replacement, displacement, and contradiction), were encountered at one time or another. In an overview of the encounters, three points can be made.

First, in those cases in which color was not used to mark a significant feature of social interaction, some other facet of material expression was employed, even if verbal expression (i.e. words on signs) often appeared, as well. Organizational size, for example, was generally marked not by color but rather by the use of physical volume and ground coverage. In differentiation among retail establishments, where color was insignificant, the goods displayed in the shop windows bore an indexical relation to the goods for sale within.

Second, where color was used, it was always reinforced or amplified by other facets of material expression. Organizations availed themselves of architectural style, composition of materials, physical size, and territorial arrangement as well as color. Some of the associations of facets found in the study area are the common currency of everyday observation. We recognize that Classical, Neo-Classical, and Renaissance architectural styles are freely exploited by organizations of high status, power, or authority. Banks, civic buildings, public monuments, educational institutions, major hotels, and expensive stores afforded examples of the use of this communicative resource. Such organizations were also the ones

that built the largest physical forms, occupied the largest
territory and employed the most expensive materials. This was the
case, as predicted by theory, even where they could have made do
with much less.

It should be added that change in the style of bank and civic
architecture to modern Functionalist designs was also observable in
the study area. With the change, other features of material form
which had complemented or reinforced the "meaning" of earlier styles
have remained much the same. Major banks and public buildings are
still physically large and territorially extensive, they use
expensive materials and they maintain their simple, almost
monochromatic, color schemes. It is as if one feature had been
allowed to evolve, perhaps reflecting new social relations, only
under the condition that the features which had complemented its
original form be allowed to maintain a proper context.

Third, in the special case of one color, its occurrence in
nature seemed to have a strong bearing on its facade use. As we
discovered in chapter IV, the color green was used less often in all
values and chroma than were the hues closest to it, yellow and blue.
In most situations the color green on a facade was not significantly
related to any of the organizational characteristics with which
several colors taken together were found to be identified. Data
available from our analysis suggest that this was not simply a
matter of omission. Plant use was closely associated with all the
relations in which the color green on facades was not involved. By
itself plant use was a good measure of functional and status
differentiation. Organizations of greater formality tended to
maintain plants or even small gardens near their facades. Banks and
civic institutions did not make use of plants as often as churches
and high-status hotels and restaurants, but they still used them
more often than did the organizations in low-status groups.

It is as though green as an element of a facade's appearance
purposely went unrealized in order that plants could be used as an
alternative marker. Some observers have explained the
under-representation of green by appealing to a stricture current in
design circles which maintains that the color should not to be
employed in exterior designs because it will clash with the greens
of the natural environment. This is a curious twist of logic for
surely the same argument would exclude blues, white, grays, and
browns from facades lest they clash with the colors of the sky,
clouds, lakes, the soil, and other natural features. It might be
more helpful to note that plants and gardens require costly care.
There is a risk that green on a facade would be seen as a cheap
imitation, comparable to the use of plastic flora.

CHAPTER VI

ALTERNATIVE INTERPRETATIONS

The dedication of the present monograph to purposes of exploration requires us to compare the interpretation offered in chapter V with its major competitors, and to address a number of issues which might seem to limit the validity of this project's conception of communication. The following pages respond to these necessities.

Theories of Semiotics and Symbology

Two features distinguishing this project's approach from others which have sought to explain the same phenomena are (1) the care with which it establishes social interaction as the context within which communication occurs, and (2) its conception of communication as a process in which any human action--including the use of material objects--may be involved. The first feature sets the project's model apart from theories put forward in semiotics and symbology. To maintain that these theories completely ignore social context would be to misrepresent their position, but it is clear from our discussion in chapter I of the assumptions lying behind their interpretations that the analytical emphasis in both semiotics and symbology is directed toward assessing the meaning of objects in action as if they could be removed from their interactional milieu.

If carried to an extreme, the models of semiotics and symbology lead to a catalog theory of the meaning of objects, as though we could look up any object in a dictionary where its possible meanings would be listed along with their "etymology" and examples of their use. From the point of view of this project's model an appropriate reference source would be something on the order of a market appraiser's manual. We would look up a context and then follow guidelines for arriving at the significance of behavioral and artifactual features associated with particular interactions. To recall a thesis from chapter I, the semiotic and symbolist points of view are predicated upon a model of communication as transmission. In the model presented in this project communication is a process of negotiation and exchange. To be sure, one must concede that in certain circumstances the process of negotiation, exchange, and transaction may be practically one of transmission, especially in cases where action is highly routinized and well practiced. Nevertheless, from this point of view negotiation is always the more general process. Accordingly, semiotic appraisals, in which human communication is presented as symbolic transmission, is subsumed under an enlarged and converted conception of human communication. The use of so-called symbols is seen as a special case of communication.

At the same time we must acknowledge that the reduction of symbolic explanations to communicational ones is a risky form of theoretical imperialism for so youthful a model. The heurmeneutics of symbology are well developed in some areas of study, while the potential of this project's approach to problems in the same areas has hardly begun to be realized. For this reason, it may be difficult to see the advantages of this wider conception. Still, two can be pointed out here.

First, the conception enhances our sensitivity to what may be considered a symbol in the first place. Traditional symbolic analysis has been applied to objects and actions at two extremes: those which pertain to clearly exceptional human accomplishments such as literature, architecture, the visual arts, and religious rites, or those which have to do with relatively mundane affairs, such as responses to kinship, table manners, and everyday dress. It has tended to ignore the middle ground of human action, arbitrarily circumscribing the actions and artifacts that can be considered symbolic. Our conception of human communication makes no arbitrary distinctions. Any artifact and any action can be "symbolic," according to its function in some particular interaction.

Second, this project's conception of communication places the idea of the "symbolic" in a new light. Depending upon the theorist, symbolism is seen as a manifestation of the deep-seated psychological properties of the individual, or as a property of group adaptations, or perhaps as an attainment of human thought and culture which distinguishes humanity from all other forms of life. Our conception maintains that behavior conceived as "symbolic" is of significance only insofar as it relates to continuing patterns of observable human action. The propagation of interaction may be rooted in the imperatives of group survival or psychological self-fulfillment but we must not confuse these teleological or ontological possibilities with the mechanisms through which they are realized in interaction.

When we move the discussion into the realm of color use, we recognize immediately that the term symbolic can be applied to the patterns discovered in this study. We could say, in keeping with semiotic thought, that colors symbolize the social relations with which they are associated. If this idea of symbolism were to be applied exhaustively to the data of the present study, we might arrive at an explanation little different, superficially, from the one put forward in chapter V. Color's value as a classifying principle would still reveal itself. Yet our understanding of the more general axioms guiding color use would be quite different. A semiotic analysis would assign color to the status of an object of study in its own right independent of the interactional contexts within which it is found. Once patterns of color use were established, a symbolist would seek to explain their relation to social forms in terms of precedent, imitation, and convention. Achromatic tones, for example, because of their past and present association with institutions of authority and control, would be seen as symbols of power and authority. Explanations of other color attributes would follow the same logic.

This project insists that the symbolist's method be turned on end. We must first analyze social forms to see what they require or imply for communicational (i.e. "symbolic") behavior. It may be convenient to think of achromatic tones as symbolization of power but to do so limits the generality of the analysis in at least two ways. First, isolating color as an analytic object so as to construct what might be termed "a semiotic of color," overlooks the fact that color is only one component of material expression. To understand the use of color we must understand its properties in relation to those of other components of material expression. Any analysis which fails to consider the complementarity of components can easily go astray. We must not arbitrarily isolate color for analysis, as symbolists are tempted to do. Second, it is difficult for the symbolist to relate color use in one realm of human action to that in another. It is too easy to regard domains of symbolic action as independent and unconnected, losing sight of the fact that patterns of color use are related by the on-going process of human interaction rather than by physical similarity alone.

The Language Analogy

While this project's conception of communication stands in contrast to those of semiotics and symbology on the basis of the priority it assigns to social interaction as context, it differs from another widely accepted approach to communicational problems on the basis of its tenet that communication is a process in which any human action--including the use of material objects--may be involved This tenet specifically challenges a communication-as-language assumption made by many scholars.

Colloquially, the term communication is taken to apply only to verbal expression, or language. This is a natural occurence given the importance of verbal expression in everyday life, but it has had an unfortunate effect on attempts at theory building. When scholars have sought to suggest that some non-verbal form of action communicates, in whatever sense, they have almost automatically drawn an analogy between that action and language. Hence authors produce articles and books titled "The Language of Clothes," "The Language of Architecture," "The Language of Art," "The Language of Landscape," and "The Language of Visual Communication." There is no question that language, as a prototypical form of communication, can support some of these analogies. The hermeneutics of language are well developed, and along with a specialized terminology developed for language study, can be adapted for application to a varied body of phenomena. In most cases, the analogy is enlightening. Concepts such as syntax, vocabulary, grammar, idiom, and dialect add to our appreciation of communication in other modes. Language analogies have provided insights into the structure of human action that might not have been made available in other ways.

It is helpful in many ways to conceive of color in the cityscape as language, or still further, to view the entire physical city as language or "text." Our attention is drawn to nuances of urban form through the subtleties of linguistic or textual interpretation. We begin to see urban analysis as a study in iconography. The concepts of metaphor, metonymy, homonymy, and simile even seem to take on the status of explanations when applied to the elements of urban form. If nothing else, these ideas lead to an appreciation of the many levels on which a "text," such as that of the city, can be "read."

Notwithstanding, as noted in chapter I, there has been vigorous debate over these analogies. The principal argument against their use is that architecture, art, and clothing do not meet the criteria, set primarily by logical positivists, which must be met before any system of human action can be called a true language. First, they have no grammar by which ill-formed utterances can be distinguished from well-formed utterances. Second, there is no way of establishing the truth conditions necessary to determine if an expression means something.[1] From our discussion of the assumptions of linguistic theory in chapter I, it is evident that these two conditions may be excessively restrictive even for language, but they must be faced and dealt with.

---

1. John Casey and Roger Scruton, "Modern Charlatanism, III: Frozen Labyrinths: Roland Barthes," *The Cambridge Review* 98 (1976):87-93.

Proponents of the language analogy have justified their
position by maintaining that while art, architecture, and clothing
are not language, they are very close to it. They say that the
linguistic model is the best approximation available. These
scholars also argue that in the history of science slightly
inappropriate analogies and metaphors have often promoted progress;
their pursuit has even led to new paradigms of scientific inquiry,
despite the fact that their initial suppositions were somewhat
flawed.[2]

This project agrees that we have benefitted from language
analogies, but it also maintains that there should be doubt as to
how beneficial they may be in the future. The sense of misgiving
derives less from a distrust of the employment of analogy than from
an awareness of the limitations of contemporary understanding of
language. As a result of our previous questioning of assumptions in
linguistic theory, we can appreciate that there is no assurance that
the prevailing conception of language can sustain the weight of
these analogies indefinitely. To go further, the analogies obscure
the fact that language and other forms of action are part of a more
general process, for which language, by itself, is not an ideal or
even appropriate model.

Language, together with the many forms of non-verbal
expression, including gesture, sartorial adornment, art and
architecture, can all be conceived of as parts of a more
encompassing process, that of communication. We are warned,
accordingly, against comparing any two or more of these components
analogically, metaphorically, or otherwise if doing so leads us into
overlooking the possibility that they are compatible as complements
at a higher level of generalization. Recognizing that they are
complements, in the sense of their all being part of the process of
human communication, we are given reason to expect that the use of
architectural forms in communication will not be very much like the
use of language. We find ourselves open to the possibility that the
physical properties which underlie their use are quite different.
From our discussion of optionality in chapter V, we can anticipate
that these differences will have consequences in the negotiation of
an interaction.

There are great advantages to viewing so much of human action,
including the use of material forms, as part of the process of human

---

2. A case for the language analogy is made by Chris Abel in "The Language
Analogy in Architectural Theory and Criticism; Some Remarks in the Light of
Wittgenstein's Linguistic Relativism," *Architectural Association Quarterly* 12
(1980):39-47.

communication. We can simplify our analysis, do away with unnecessary assumptions, and focus on an appropriate and more manageable object of study, that is, the propagation of human interaction. While analogies to language have clarified the ways in which different components of the communication process resemble one another, the theory of human communication, through the concept of optionality (as applied both at the level of linkage networks and at the level of the individual linkage) has the capacity to systematize these observations. We can begin to appreciate the importance of lateral associations--the simultaneous functioning of many components in an interaction.

In some lateral associations, color complements language. For example, in interactions associated with access to power, control, authority--or to high-status, prestigious groups--language usage is generally prescribed in great detail. Legal codes, the rules of order for legislative debate, books of worship, and canons of etiquette all specify how language is to be used in formal interactions involving access to authority. It is also the case that in these situations color use tends to follow definite strictures. Such interactions are typically framed in very simple color schemes involving achromatic or monochromatic tones (generally of low value). If other or more vivid colors are introduced they generally frame the social distinctions or roles found among the participants in the interaction.

Lateral associations, whether inclusive of color use or not, are abundantly represented in everyday life. Little more than cursory observation is required to confirm that there are significant consistencies in the way language is associated with clothing, body behavior, elements of interior design, and components of architecture to frame interaction. In fact it should be no surprise to find oneself independently discovering types of lateral association (i.e. evidence that optionality is regularly operative in the propagation of interaction). Under the terms of this project's model these types can be appreciated as significant structural features of communication.

The Idea of Imageability

As indicated in chapter V, an issue that must be confronted with respect to color in public spaces has to do with imageability, that is, with the proposition that some visual presentations are noticed and remembered more readily (have a greater imageability) than others. The idea of imageability has been brought into prominence over the last two or so decades by scholars intent on understanding how people perceive large urban environments as a

whole and in parts, how they conceptualize information drawn from
their experiences within these environments, and how they develop
organizational mnemonics which guide their behavior within these
localities.[3] These scholars have had some success in relating
behavior to the imageability of urban built environments, that is,
to the relative ease with which people are able to use buildings and
other physical objects as markers of territories and neighborhoods
in which their behavior takes place.

However, this approach to the analysis of urban experience
fails for the same reason that semiotic theories of physical form
fail. It assumes that people abstract images from the situations in
which they have played a part, assigning meaning to them independent
of interactional context. From the point of view of the present
project's concept of communication, investigations of this type
commit the error of selecting the wrong object of study. In
centering their own attention upon schemas of the environment which
are presumed to transcend the immediate context of action in which
people are involved, the authors are prevented from realizing that
social interaction is the pivot around which people's "subjective"
evaluations and use of material forms revolve.

There can be little doubt that people do develop impressions
of large sections of an urban setting, and that they act upon these
broad generalizations in some interactions. Of the great number of
linkages that are established each day in a large city, we can be
sure that some will almost necessitate that people's images and
broad-based socio-environmental mnemonics be used. However, to ask
people to evaluate their environment independent of the context
within which they find themselves, as many scholars do in their
surveys, is all too likely to produce responses that only reflect
the form of the question asked. An answer may be simply an artifact
of interaction, helping to sustain the interview and to propagate
the series of interactions of which the interview is part, while
doing little to reveal the interactional components of the
interviewee's social environment.

People may say that their perception of a city like Chicago is
centered around an image of its skyscrapers. This image itself may
be the source of a good deal of civic pride and prejudice, but the
recollections in which it appears may serve people no differently

---

3 . Kenneth Boulding, *The Image: Knowledge in Life and Society* (Ann Arbor:
University of Michigan Press, 1956); Kevin Lynch, *The Image of the City*
(Cambridge, Mass.: MIT Press, 1960); Roger M. Downs and David Stea, *Image and
Environment. Cognitive Mapping and Spatial Behavior* (Chicago: Aldine Publishing
Company, 1973); John H. Sims and Duane D. Baumann, *Human Behavior and the
Environment: Interactions Between Man and His Physical World* (Chicago: Maaroufa
Press, 1974); and Thomas F. Saarinen, *Environmental Planning: Perception and
Behavior* (Boston: Houghton-Mifflin Company, 1976).

from the way a discussion of the weather, in the course of a casual
encounter, serves them. Mention of the weather, as is well known,
can be significant only in so far as it signals a person's attitude
toward continued interaction. The perceived state of the weather
does not really matter. Similarly, what people recall of their
images of Cleveland, New England, or Chicago may have only an
immediate interactional significance. They may not contribute much
toward an understanding of other interactions.

If these objections may be raised to the thinking about image
and imageability found in discussions of landmarks, layouts and the
like, they apply no less to arguments that might seek to dispose of
color use in public spaces by reducing it to a simple problem of
image making. It might be asked, cannot the color on facades be
explained as the result of a constant quest by organizations for
readily imageable color combinations and arrangements? This
project's position is that the quest may be real enough, at least
for some organizations under some conditions, but that an adequate
understanding neither of its pursuit nor of its consequences can be
expected without establishing at the outset the interactional
context in which it occurs.

The Question of Efficiency

In chapter V, both in the discussion of choice among modes of
expression and of choice among facets of the material mode of
expression, various reasons were given that might justify the
preferences of participants, according to type of interaction. Yet
nowhere were the possible justifications equated with efficiency.
If at all, the use of material expression (among the modes) or of
color (among the facets) is "efficient" only in the sense that its
use best fits the requirements of an immediate social situation.
Sometimes its use will require a lesser expenditure of energy in the
propagation of interaction, and at other times just the opposite.
Efficiency is relative to context. For anything resembling a
defensible judgement on efficiency, furthermore, one must often take
into account, as context, a series of interactions which might
stretch far into the past and, by projection, far into the future,
while touching upon a large number of complementary interactions.

If we see this whole series of interactions as relevant to the
question of efficiency, then we have opened up the possibility that
efficiency will have to be ascertained anew for each term of the
series. To participants in one set of interactions, the forms used
in some other set might seem to be highly inefficient, representing
a squandering of resources. But, upon reappraisal with reference to
the interaction itself, the use of these resources, however

profligate their allocation might seem from without, may be demonstrably required. As a result of the conflicting standards applied to resource allocation by different frames of interaction, it is inevitable that contradictions will arise.

It may also appear to some members of society that others are using resources in the furtherance of interactions which impede or conflict with the general social good. In our society the automobile, the single family home, and many appliances of convenience present the spectacle of resource use of this kind. Undeniably, these artifacts are in many ways inefficient. They consume large amounts of material and energy resources and create ecological problems which could be prevented through the adoption of other modes of transportation, different types of group habitation, or alternative habits of personal consumption.

We must notice, however, that artifacts which represent the inefficient use of some resources are tied directly to forces which lie behind social form. To deny people the cars, homes, and appliances with which they establish their identities without providing them with some acceptable substitute would be to disrupt the conventions which guide the smooth flow of human action. A major renegotiation of roles, values, and norms would be required. Since social actors have no assurance that such a renegotiation would turn in their favor, resistance to change is understandable. People continue to use "inefficient" forms even when presented with "rational" reasons for discarding them. Generally speaking, changes of form are gradual, occurring only when people have assurance that they will not be deprived of their social roles and identity without compensation.

In Thorstein Veblen's theory of the leisure class[4] we find an oft-cited indictment for inefficiency. Veblen was alarmed at the way status symbols had come to consume resources to the point of waste. Coining the term "conspicuous consumption," he gave vent to his frustration with modern societies where subscription to pecuniary canons of taste serve to set off elite classes. From the point of view of this study, we must separate Veblen's observations on social form from his critiques. As an observer, he had things to say about consumption, display, and social opinion that still must be admired for their portrayal of human communication in action.

As a critic Veblen saw the displays and associated activities as wasteful since they did hardly more than protect an antiquated class which, as he saw its members, could lay little claim to

---

4. Thorstein Veblen, *The Theory of the Leisure Class: An Economic Study of the Evolution of Institutions* (New York: MacMillan and Co., 1905).

usefulness. He failed to consider that while at one level
ostentatious displays of class affiliation may seem inefficient, at
another level they may become recognizable highly efficient means
for realizing social control. To do away with these "inefficient"
forms would almost certainly disrupt the very interactions in which
these forms seem to play such a wasteful part. Also, because these
interactions might support still other interactions at other levels,
their loss might lead to a wholesale rending of the web of social
action.

It is always easy for a social participant to abstract from
the particular series of interactions through which his or her
identity is established, so as to criticize the inefficiency or
seeming folly of the forms by which other participants express their
identity. Unfortunately, such criticism often accomplishes no more
than to buttress the identity of the critic. People are often quick
to recognize the superfluity of those interactions in which they
have no desire to participate, and with regard to these, to
discover a margin between the "decorative" elaboration of an
interaction and the essential value of the interaction. Their
criticism can extend to "taste"and "value" generally, and to
comprehensive questions of "good" and "bad," as criticism is
directed to the form of buildings people occupy, to their choice of
occupation, hobby, music, clothing, and vocabulary, to their kinesic
or proxemic bearing, and so forth.

This project is committed, in short, to an extreme form of
cultural relativism. The conception of communication developed here
denies that questions of taste and value have an absolute
foundation, holding rather that these judgements are validated
socially and culturally. The standard against which they must be
assessed is their relation to the genealogy or propagation of social
interaction. Their significance derives from the ways in which they
are used to establish class distinctions, for example, and how these
class distinctions relate to a viable system of interaction. Usage
with regard to costumes, patterns of conduct, manner of speech, and
physical settings are only the means by which social actors realize
their identities. People apply criticism to what they perceive as
deviations from appropriate social forms, forms that often serve as
their own means of control. At the extreme they will refuse to
interact with people who refuse to conform to their standards.

As with appropriateness and good taste and high value, so with
efficiency: the meaning of all are context dependent. The
properties of communicational forms must be taken into account
simply for what they are: the limiting conditions of a repertoire

through which the process of communication is realized under the imperatives of continued social action. There is no property either of a mode of expression or of a facet of some mode that necessitates a particular use in interaction, or that determines its use to be efficient independent of these imperatives.

The Role of the Architect

It will have been surprising to many readers, and perhaps even offensive to some, that the role of the architect has been omitted from the present study. For the author, who is not unacquainted with the literature of architectural design, criticism, and history, the omission was made, and then held to throughout the execution of the study, to make one point unequivocally: that from this project's point of view, the architect has less to add to our understanding of the physical city than we are often led to believe. The position on the role of the architect is parallel to that taken on the great writer by students of socio-linguistics and on the clothing designer by some writers in sociology and anthropology.

Over the last two decades the field of socio-linguistics has made important contributions to our understanding of language use and change.[5] Semantic, pragmatic, and syntactic characteristics of language have been associated with patterns of class and ethnic affiliation as well as with social control and coordination. From the socio-linguistic standpoint the work of a great writer has little to do with our more general understanding of the social meaning of language. The two are related, but it would rarely be the case that an author's literary production would be the principal source of a particular linguistic change. Linguistic change is more likely to be associated with fundamental alterations in patterns of social integration. We can assert that the architect's role with regard to the built environment is like that of the writer's to language. The two are related, but not in the way the architectural profession typically would have us believe. Sometimes an architect has a profound effect on the appearance of the built environment, but generally this is not the case.

Similarly, sociological and anthropological studies of clothing have pointed out strong relations between socio-cultural

---

5. A survey of this literature would include Roger Bell, *Sociolinguistics: Goals, Approaches, and Problems* (New York: St. Martin's Press, 1976); Basil Bernstein, *Class, Codes, and Control: Theoretical Studies Towards Sociology of Language* (New York: Schocken Books, 1971); Norbert Dittmar, *A Critical Survey of Sociolinguistics: Theory and Application* (New York: St. Martin's Press, 1976); Dell Hymes, *Foundations in Sociolinguistics: An Ethnographic Approach* (Philadelphia: University of Pennsylvania Press, 1974); and William Labov, *Language in the Inner City: Studies in the Black English Vernacular* (Philadelphia: University of Pennsylvania Press, 1972) as well as *Sociolinguistic Patterns* (Philadelphia: University of Pennsylvania Press, 1972).

conditions and the way people dress.[6] Although scholars of the subject have concerned themselves with the role of the fashion designer, it has been generally for reasons other than an understanding of the underlying dynamics of dress. They recognize that the clothing designer, like the great writer or storyteller, is limited in the ways he or she can influence prevailing patterns of social expression.

Clothing designers are constrained by rather unyielding social conventions. They can manipulate their elements or push them to the limits, but an understanding of why designers sometimes do just that (perhaps for career advancement) leaves untouched the question, for example, why policemen wear rigorously prescribed uniforms while most students do not. The architect is just as constrained by convention, even while he or she exercises creativity in the design of buildings. The architect helps shape the physical city but every communicating individual does the same, most in only a very small way.

With a general perspective on the physical city maintained, one could, of course, approach the relation between architect and client or between architect and a general public as one of communication. A communication-based interpretation would be a distinct departure from the mainstream of architectural literature. In such a departure, which holds the promise of being exceptionally interesting, lines of investigation opened up in the present study would be greatly extended; complex linkages merely indicated here would be explored. Given the sensitivity of this research frame to social context and its openness to the implication of all types of human action in the communication process, we can be certain in advance that the architect's role would be rescued from its customary and unsatisfying isolation.

---

6. Much attention has been devoted to understanding the relation between clothing and social forms. Some sources which have faced this question include: Ernestine Carter, *The Changing World of Fashion* (New York: Putnam's, 1977); Rachel H. Kemper, *Costume* (New York: Newsweek Books, 1977); James Laver, *The Concise History of Costume and Fashion* (New York: Abrams, 1969); Alison Lurie, *The Language of Clothes* (New York: Random House, 1981); Geoffrey Squires, *Dress and Society, 1560-1970* (New York: Viking, 1974); Doreen Yarwood, *The Encyclopedia World Costume* (New York: Scribners, 1978); Dick Hebdige, *Subculture: The Meaning of Style* (New York: Methuen, Inc., 1979); and Ted Polhemus and Lynn Proctor, *Fashion and Anti-Fashion: Anthropology of Clothing and Adornment* (London: Thames and Hudson, 1978).

CHAPTER VII

TOWARD A COMMUNICATION-BASED THEORY OF THE BUILT ENVIRONMENT

A monograph such as this, in seeking to encompass so large a subject, must necessarily fail to address some issues relevant to its theme. Some of these issues involve problems which could only be resolved upon completion of research projects beyond the scope of the present study. However, although exposition of these issues at this juncture would prove inconclusive, the findings of the present project do have a bearing on the manner in which these matters might profitably be investigated in future research.

Of the many issues that suggest themselves when we discuss communication in the broad terms advocated in this dissertation, many fall within the traditional domain of urban geography. Such issues, including those relating to color, pertain to the physical city, and are amenable to analysis in terms of the theory of human communication. In other words, the physical city can be at least partly explained as a cultural artifact in terms of the material dimensions of the process of human communication, a mode of conceptualization that points toward a modified paradigm for the study of urban geography. It may be anticipated that this paradigm will subsume at least the themes set out in the following pages.

Future Research into the Physical City

It has already been suggested that our understanding of the process of human communication might profit from the application of our analysis to other facets of architectural form: for example, architectural style, material composition, and physical size. Empirical analysis would probably reveal patterns of no little importance to our understanding of human communication, as a result of which the present study could be evaluated with reference to a more complete knowledge of the properties conditioning the use of physical objects in communication. However, if the analysis served only to fill in the cells of a matrix the algebraic solution to which we suspected we already knew, it might turn out to be a less than profitable undertaking. In the circumstances, it would probably be more effective to consider departures based upon less evident features of our conception of communication.

The Evidence of Cultural Form

The departures to be considered all revolve around the primary characteristics of the conception of communication that we have adopted. These include sensitivity to the context of human action and a willingness to categorize a wide range of types of behavior as communicational. Yet the argument which clarifies these proposed departures stems from neither one nor the other of these fundamental properties. Instead, it arises from the juxtaposition of the two within our idea of communication itself.

This paper has maintained from the beginning that we can only know culture effectively through its system of communication and by the evidence of behavior and artifact that living systems continually generate, use, reuse, and discard. This position implicitly disputes the nature of the evidence upon which much social theory has been constructed. It questions both the status of the facts and observations used in social explanation and the character of the inferences that can be drawn from them. It also directs our attention continually to the communicational filter through which human action passes. The process of communication is interposed between social forces that we cannot observe and the action and artifacts that we can. This does not mean that the forces producing observable human action are controlled by the process of communication or that communication is the fundamental animating force in society. Nor does it imply acceptance of a behavioristic mode of thought. It seeks only to relate communication to human interaction, which has itself been the principal object of traditional social theory. Nonetheless, this project's conception of communication is capable of furnishing useful insights into the material and behavioral expression of social forces, while warning us against overlooking the fact that verbal and gestural action and physical objects are complementary parts of a more general process of communication. Yet, although they can reinforce, substitute for, and replace one another, it must never be forgotten that, if removed from their context, actions ad objects lose their meaning.

The various social theories interpret interaction in different ways: as cultural or group adaptations, as the juxtaposition of open, living systems in time and space, as a function of a society's means of production, or as the realization of ideological imperatives. But no matter which of these styles of explanation may prove effective, all must concede that the imperatives of social organization can only be realized communicationally. No matter what the unseen motives of the individual or the intangible necessities of social participation, both are filtered through the communication process as they acquire material expression. Both members and observers of a culture can know it only through the actions of its individual members and the material forms they use.

As we prepare a prospectus for future research into the built environment from the standpoint of urban geography, there are two areas where the application of this broad-based conception of communication seems to hold potential for advances in our understanding. First, the evidence provided by the material aspect of the communication process can be put to new uses both at the level of the individual (when it is germane to the fields of behavioral geography and environmental psychology) and at the level of social institutions (when it bears on the themes of social and cultural geography). Second, the theoretical implications of viewing the creation of the physical city as the result of an all-encompassing communication-based process call for a reappraisal of the nature of explanation in urban geography.

Additions to the Agenda of Urban Geography

Artifacts and the Individual: Public and Private Displays of Identity

The conception of communication developed in this project promotes understanding of the ways in which people express their identities, social roles, or class or ethnic affiliations as they inhabit the urban environment. In several contributions on this topic, Goffman has developed a fruitful method for the analysis of the behavior, speech, and costuming of individuals in a variety of everyday situations.[1] In fact, the idea of public displays of identity, the study of costumes and facades, and the way people present themselves to others in commonplace, formal, or ritual settings can be seen as a heuristic kernel from which a productive research strategy might be developed. At the point at which the individual commmits his or her identity to material expression, it is possible to posit a rough equivalence between the resulting physical objects and the social characteristics of that individual. By acquiring information about both social form and its corresponding physical artifacts, it would appear to be possible to give tentative definition to some of the pragmatic relations that animate the use of material expression in the communication process.

1. Erving Goffman, *Behavior in Public Places: Notes on the Social Organization of Gatherings* (New York: Free Press, 1963); *The Presentation of Self in Everyday Life* (Garden City, N.Y.: Doubleday, 1959); and *Strategic Interaction* (Philadelphia: University of Pennsylvania Press, 1969).

Although people express their identities through costumes, it would be a mistake to see these costumes as comprising only clothing. A person's "costume" is a communicational envelope whose dimensions are defined by verbal and gestural action as well as by clothing and physical objects. Its interpretation has also been the subject of semiotic analysis. Insight into the "self" as it is expressed materially has been provided by both Sebeok and Singer.[2] Singer's discussion of the relation between individuals (and particular social groups) and the emblems of community life is particularly relevant to some traditional themes of social and urban historical geography.[3]

Our preferred conceptualization of communication is also useful in explaining how people express their identities through the physical objects they gather around themselves, a topic recently investigated by Csikszentmihalyi and Rochberg-Halton.[4] These authors report interviews with 315 members of 82 families in Chicago and Evanston, Illinois concerning the use of personal objects found in the home. They make the point that, while everyone seems to understand that personal objects can serve as status symbols, they overlook the fact that these symbols are often used to project an image which actually disguises the self. In fact, the possession of many personal objects can only be understood in relation to the way they allow individuals to build up a personal image of the self; that is, they help people define who they are. This explanation of the use of objects belies the simple explanation that they are always part of a public display.

This conclusion is compatible with the conception of communication used in this study, which maintains that individuals can establish their identities communicationally, that is through action and the use of objects. Regardless of whether these actions and objects are displayed in public or private, they always retain a certain self-adapting quality. While they may be exhibited in public, they are also employed to realize a personal identity. It

2. Thomas A. Sebeok, "The Semiotic Self," in *The Sign and Its Masters,* ed. T.A. Sebeok (Austin, Tx.: University of Texas Press, 1979); Milton Singer, "Signs of the Self: An Exploration in Semiotic Anthropology," *American Antropologist* 82 (September 1980):488-507, "On the Symbolic and Historic Structure of an American Identity," *Ethos* 5 (1977):431-454, "On the Semiotics of Indian Identity," *American Journal of Semiotics* 1 (1981):85-126, and "Personal and Social Identity in Dialogue," in *Approaches to the Development of the Self,* ed. Benjamin Lee (New York: Plenum, 1981).

3. Milton Singer, "Emblems of Identity: A Semiotic Exploration," in *Symbols in Anthropology,* ed. J. Maquet (Malibu, Cal.: Undena Publications, 1981).

4. Mihaly Csikszentmihalyi and Eugene Rochberg-Halton, *The Meaning of Things: Domestic Symbols and the Self* (New York: Cambridge University Press, 1981).

must not be forgotten that artifacts are intimately involved in the integration of the self into society.

Material Forms and the Genealogy of Institutional Control

Although the process of communication as here envisaged is capable of mediating between any social force and its physical expression, the model might be particularly effective if applied to the analysis of social power, control, and authority. These concepts have always figured prominently in all branches of urban studies, including urban geography, because these forces and the institutions in which they manifest themselves, are the organizations most capable of molding the morphology of cities.

Scholars such as Michel Foucault have often pointed out that the disposition of power and the instruments of its control, however they are manifested, are keys to the understanding both of social organization and the mode of its expression.[5] It seems that, regardless of the social theory adopted, there is always a need to understand the workings of institutions of societal control, of the means by which culture comes to exert restraints that prevent the war of one against the many. Foucault's concepts of social form are no different. To appreciate his archaeology of knowledge, we must also take account of the archaeologies of social interaction and of communication. What makes Foucault's ideas appealing, though, is that they anticipate the type of analysis which might be accomplished by applying this project's conception of communication to the structures of societal power.

Foucault's concept of "the genealogy of power" might serve as an interesting starting point for evaluating the use of social artifacts in the city.[6] It might prove enlightening to try to trace

---

5. Michel Foucault has developed these ideas in a number of works including *The Archaeology of Knowledge* (London: Tavistock Publications, 1972); *Language, Counter-Memory, Practice: Selected Essays and Interviews* (Ithaca, N.Y.: Cornell University Press, 1977); *The Order of Things: An Archaeology of the Human Sciences* (New York: Pantheon Books, 1970); and *Power/Knowledge: Selected Interviews and Other Writings, 1972-1977* (New York: Pantheon Books, 1980).
   For a discussion of Foucault's philosophy and writings see Alan Sheridan, *Michel Foucault: The Will to Truth* (New York: Tavistock Publications, 1980).

6. Foucault's genealogy is not a search for origins, rather it is the cultivation of a sensitivity to the essential variability of beginning and existence. As he states, "A genealogy of values, morality, asceticism, and knowledge will never confuse itself with a quest for their "origins," will never neglect as inaccessible the vicissitudes of history. On the contrary, it will cultivate the details and accidents that accompany every beginning; it will be scrupulously attentive to their petty malice; it will await their emergence, once unmasked, as the face of the other. Wherever it is made to go, it will not be reticent--in "excavating the depths," in allowing time for these elements to escape from a labyrinth where no truth had ever detained them" *(Language, Counter-Memory, Practice: Selected Essays and Interviews,* edited and with an introduction by Donald F. Bouchard [Ithaca, N.Y.: Cornell University Press, 1977], p. 144). Thus, "Genealogy does not pretend to go back in time to restore an unbroken continuity that operates beyond the dispersion of forgotten things; its duty is not to demonstrate that the past actively exists in the present, that it continues secretly to animate the present, having imposed a predetermined form

this genealogy of power in terms of interaction structure. Do the material forms which frame interaction and mediate in social negotiations also reflect the operation of this genealogy? Could the expression of this genealogy employ the resources of material expression in communication to its advantage? Some of the evidence we have collected in the course of this analysis suggests that such hypotheses would repay testing.

Identity and Control

Even if it is unnecessary--and in any case would be premature at this stage of research--to assert that interaction and its concomitant material expression trace out a genealogy of power in society, or that interaction is always directed toward the integration of the self into society, it seems likely that our analysis could be extended to encompass the idea of identity as well as that of control. It might be hypothesized, for example, that whenever a new type of interaction occurs, it seeks to distinguish itself from other interactions by employing new combinations of physical forms. In this connection, it would be interesting to investigate the ways in which new industries and businesses select costumes by which to portray their corporate identities, and how they use material expression to frame the activity of their employees. It would probably prove highly instructive to determine the extent to which an organization exploiting an industrial, technological, or economic innovation (such as computer and electronic technologies, financial innovations, or new concepts in marketing) patterns its new costume on precedents set by the organizations generating the innovation, as well as how the new pattern diverges from those of its predecessors. Observations of this order could be made at any juncture in history where a new social class came into existence, with the object of determining if the emerging class selected a new "costume" (including all the material and architectonic goods it gathered around itself) to set itself apart from other classes?

The emergence of new states and new governments might be investigated along similar lines. We might speculate, for example,

---

to all its vicissitudes. Genealogy does not resemble the evolution of a species and does not map the destiny of a people. On the contrary, to follow the complex course of descent is to maintain passing events in their proper dispersion; it is to identify the accidents, the minute deviations--or conversely, the complete reversals--the errors, the false appraisals, and the faulty calculations that gave birth to those things that continue to exist and have value for us; it is to discover that truth or being do not lie at the root of what we know and what we are, but the exteriority of accidents" (ibid., p. 146). Further discussion of this concept is included in the same essay from which these quotations were drawn: "Nietzsche, Genealogy, History," (ibid., pp. 139-164). Other commentary is provided by Alan Sheridan, *Foucault: The Will to Truth*, (New York: Tavistock Publications, 1980), pp. 114-120,205,220-222.

that the greater the degree to which a government constitutes a departure from what went before, the more distinctive will be the new costume it will devise for itself. We might then be suspicious of a new form of government which, while publicly promulgating a radically new ideology, continues to occupy the costume of its predecessor. Its failure to seek a new material framing for the new type of interactions it promises might suggest that it is not such a radical departure after all.

Similar considerations might apply to the propagation of utopian philosophies. To the extent that such philosophies claim to represent departures from established norms of social action, we would expect their implementation to result in the creation of new patterns and constellations of physical artifacts. These are only four of the many examples which could be studied.7 Any situation in which a new social role or interaction is defined is a potential source of relevant data.

The Urban Built Environment and Fundamental Processes of Human Action

So far we have suggested ways in which our broad conceptualization of human communication and the idea that culture can be illuminated through its system of communication might lead to a better understanding of urban form. We shall conclude our discussion by examining one further line of investigation deriving from this project's methodological stance. We have now reached the point where we can begin to evaluate the urban built environment in terms of the intrinsic processes of human thought and action (which together signify communication). This undertaking, rather than adding discrete topics to the agenda for urban geography, carries the radical implication of a need for a totally revised paradigm for continued study in this field.

While recognizing that it is satisfying to be able to rely on a conceptualization capable of framing the human use of artifacts in

---

7. Among the sources that have a direct bearing on the study of public displays of identity by organizations, two types can be discerned. The first comprises observations of the reuse of architectonic costumes, including recent summaries of contemporary phenomena such as urban homesteading, historical preservation, and urban gentrification. The second includes sources which are only indirectly relevant. It might be informative, for instance, to invite people to react verbally to various architectonic costumings, to ask them, say, whether a building is appropriate for the organization that occupies it. It might also be interesting to ascertain how the public reacts to organizational-material disguises, as when an organization dresses out of character, and thereby displays a sort of architectonic transvestism. Negative evidence afforded by organizations that failed to abide by the patterns uncovered by such an investigation would be no less informative. Study of design competitions (i.e. the selection of a costume by an organization in a formal competitive ritual) might also be pertinent. For example, the well documented design competition for the Chicago *Tribune* office tower might throw light on acceptable and unacceptable prop usage. Furthermore, it might be possible to learn something about linkages, props, organizations, and communication by studying buildings that are planned but never built. This could lead to some profitable comparative study, perhaps touching again upon utopian designs and the frequency with which they fail to be executed.

this way, it is frustrating to realize that it also makes the evaluation of their significance all the more difficult. Props are plastic; their significance is very linkage and context dependent. As we noted earlier, even when we understand the attributions of props in one interaction, we recognize that these qualities will not necessarily (or even probably) be carried into subsequent exchanges. They relate to human interaction, involving in turn displays of identity, mechanisms for the integration of the self into society, and the material expression of societal control. Nonetheless, there is some likelihood that investigations directed toward framing some very broad linkages will prove valuable to the study of other, narrower linkages. Thus information gained from studying the correlation of prop and role in one setting will probably have continuing significance in other contexts even though both the props themselves and their attributes are likely to change.

This anticipated continuity results from the ways in which props come to serve as memory devices in interactions. It seems that the complex, mixed-modal patterning of communicative events within the urban built environment is somehow underpinned by complicated, associative patterns of thought and reasoning. People readily recognize constellations of material and behavioral cues which serve to frame a wide variety of social interactions, occurring sometimes in rapid succession. They seem almost always able to grasp the integrated structures that furnish the context of their actions. The ease with which people accomplish this feat suggests the operation of an effective mechanism of substitution.

This project views props as in some ways analogous to metaphor and metonymy in literary theory. Many props are, in fact, used in interactions according to a metaphoric convention. Even though these props are physically very different from the aspects of interactions that they serve to define, certain generic similarities between the interaction and the class of object from which the prop is drawn allow them to be substituted for elements of the interaction. Once used, the prop becomes a gloss for these elements of interaction, while the substance of the interaction is enlivened by the ancillary characteristics of the form class from which the prop is drawn. In many ways, architectonic forms serve as metaphors, as when, say physical characteristics of size and material structure come to stand in for the size and social structure of the organization that uses them. The physical object is certainly different from the social form, yet it stands in by reason of a generic resemblance.

Other props function metonymically, their interchangeability arising from the circumstance that they are drawn from the same form-class as the element of interaction for which they are substituted. The relation is that of whole to part, or, through a synecdochic relationship, of feature to feature.

It would be misleading to maintain that all props function metaphorically or metonymically in a strict literary sense. Some come to represent linkages completely by convention. No analogy need be implied between, for example, a religious group and the church structure it comes to inhabit. The analogy is one of convention arising from use, rather than of physical or visual metaphor. Nevertheless, the processes of metaphoric and metonymic reasoning often provide insights into the interactional function of physical artifacts.

This project is not alone in according to metaphor and metonymy a larger role in social theory than they have been allowed in literary theory.[8] Current speculation has come to regard metaphor as a basic component of the thought process.[9] The basis for such conjecture derives from the associative and conceptual nature of human thought processes. Although the details need not concern us directly, the general character of these processes is important.

A long tradition of anthropological writing has emphasized that people divide reality, so to speak, into a multiplicity of categories, sometimes discrete, sometimes overlapping, which they use to evaluate their social environment and to participate in society. The world view of integrated experiential structures that results from such a division affords a way of assigning meaning to activities. These patterns and categorizations of similarities and differences may be learned slowly or new categories of significance may be devised almost spontaneously in the course of an interaction. The use of the terms metaphor and metonymy in cognitive theory are a recognition of this human propensity to categorize and classify the artifacts and experiences of life, thereby allowing interactions to

8. Many sources have taken this position including Max Black, *Models and Metaphors: Studies in Language and Philosophy* (Ithaca, N.Y.: Cornell University Press, 1962); Sheldon Sacks, ed., Special Issue on Metaphor, *Critical Inquiry*, 5 (Autumn 1978) (Republished as *On Metaphor* ed. Sheldon Sacks [Chicago: University of Chicago Press, 1979]); J. David Sapir and J. Christopher Crocker, *The Social Use of Metaphor: Essays on the Anthropology of Rhetoric* (Philadelphia: University of Pennsylvania Press, 1977); I. A. Richards, *The Philosophy of Rhetoric* (New York: Oxford University Press, 1936); Andrew Ortony, ed., *Metaphor and Thought* (Cambridge: Cambridge University Press, 1979); Paul Ricoeur, *The Rule of Metaphor: Multi-disciplinary Studies of the Creation of Meaning in Language* (Toronto: University of Toronto Press, 1977); Peter Schofer and Donald Rice, "Metaphor, Metonymy, and Synecdoche Revis(it)ed," *Semiotica* 21 (1977):121-144; and Yi-Fu Tuan, "Sign and Metaphor," *Annals of the Association of American Geographers* 68 (September 1978):363-372.

9. George Lakoff and Mark Johnson, *Metaphors We Live By* (Chicago: University of Chicago Press, 1980).

occur at many linkage levels in rapid, indeed almost simultaneous, succession. Thus in recent theory, metaphor and metonymy are posited as the processes through which categories are compared, evaluated, used, and modified. In short, metaphor is seen as a mechanism that animates the human conceptual system.

Although this project conceives of metaphor and metonymy as playing central roles in the understanding of communication and landscape, it is in no position to accept uncritically certain of the untested claims of recent literature. The insights that it can extract from its data are more limited. But, just as our conception of communication affords us the opportunity of investigating types of social control and authority through the study of their material expression in interaction processes, it also allows us to extend our analysis potentially to the point where our understanding of social communication is bounded only by our knowledge of the intrinsic properties of human thought. It enables us to recognize and define the communication processes involved in displays of identity and in the representation of power, both of which manifestations depend upon the human propensity to classify, categorize, and partition experiences and to relate them through the algebra of metaphor, analogy, and metonymy. In other words, an understanding of how material expression is involved in the communication process must involve, by implication, the most basic of human thought processes. To take this point of view is to accept a revised paradigm of study in urban and cultural geography.

Summary

Insofar as this thesis is reporting progress toward a goal it has only just begun to realize, our discussion is complete. In chapter V empirical analysis of our data afforded considerable support for the concept of communication outlined in the first two chapters. In chapter VI we related these conclusions to alternative modes of explanation of the communication process.

Finally, in this chapter we have proposed several theoretical extensions which our conception might be able to sustain, subject, of course, to future empirical investigation. First, we questioned the nature of the evidence used to make inferences about social institutions. Then, we suggested that this project's conception of communication could be used to investigate questions of individual identity and the physical morphology of institutions of social control. In this way we have added new topics to the agenda of study in urban geography. Moreover, because our conception of communication is compatible with the dynamics of human thought processes as at present understood, it is able to link the form of large-scale cultural artifacts to certain intrinsic properties of those processes. Consequently, it is able to ground our understanding of the physical city, the very structure of the urban built environment, in fundamental features of human action, interaction, and communication.

BIBLIOGRAPHY

CITED SOURCES

Abel, Chris. "The Language Analogy in Architectural Theory and Criticism; Some Remarks in the Light of Wittgenstein's Linguistic Relativism." *Architectural Association Quarterly* 12 (1980):39-47.

Agrest, Diana. "Architectural Anagrams: The Symbolic Performance of Skyscrapers." *Oppositions* 11 (Winter 1977):26-51.

Agrest, Diana and Gandelsonas, Mario. "Critical Remarks on Semiology and Architecture." *Semiotica* 9 (1974):252-271.

_____. "Semiotics and Architecture: Ideological Consumption or Theoretical Work." *Oppositions* 1 (1978):93-100.

_____. "Semiotics and the Limits of Architecture." In *A Perfusion of Signs,* pp. 90-120. Edited by Thomas A. Sebeok. Bloomington: Indiana University Press, 1977.

American Automobile Association. *Tourbook: Illinois, Indiana, Ohio.* Falls Church, Va.: The American Automobile Association, 1981.

Anderson, Stanford., ed. *On Streets.* Cambridge, Mass.: MIT Press, 1978.

Baird, George; Smith, Norris K.; Colquhoun, Alan; Rykwert, Joseph; and Moretti, Luigi. "Meaning in Architecture," *Arena, The Architectural Association Journal* 83 (1967), entire issue.

Barthes, Roland. *Elements of Semiology.* Translated by Annette Lavers and Colin Smith. New York: Hill and Wang, 1967.

Baudrillard, Jean. *Le Systeme des Objets.* Paris: Gallimard, 1968.

_____. *Pour une Critique de l'Economie Politique du Signe.* Paris: Gallimard, 1972.

Bell, Roger. *Sociolinguistics: Goals, Approaches, and Problems.* New York: St. Martin's Press, 1976.

Bernstein, Basil. *Class, Codes, and Control: Theoretical Studies Towards Sociology of Language.* New York: Schocken Books, 1971.

Birren, Faber. *Color, Form, and Space.* New York: Reinhold Publishing Co., 1961.

_____. *Color and Human Response.* New York: Van Nostrand Reinhold, 1978.

Black, Max. *Models and Metaphors. Studies in Language and Philosophy.* Ithaca, N.Y.: Cornell University Press, 1962.

Blalock, Hubert M., Jr. *Social Statistics,* 2nd ed. New York: McGraw-Hill Book Company, 1972.

Bliss, Anna Campbell. "Color Selection as a Design Decision." *American Institute of Architects Journal* 67 (October 1978):60-65.

Blomeyer, Gerald. "Architecture as a Political Sign System." *International Architect* 1 (1979):54-60.

Blomeyer, Gerald R. and Helmholtz, Rita M. "Semiotic in Architecture: A Classifying Analysis of an Architectural Object." *Semiosis 1: Zietschrift fur Semiotik und ihre Anwendungen* 1 (1976):42-51.

Bloomfield, Leonard. *Language.* New York: Henry Holt and Co., 1933.

Blumer, Herbert. *Symbolic Interactionism: Perspective and Method.* Englewood Cliffs, N.J.: Prentice-Hall, 1969.

Bonta, Juan Pablo. *Architecture and its Interpretation: A Study of Expressive Systems in Architecture.* New York: Rizzoli International Publications, Inc., 1979.

Boulding, Kenneth. *The Image: Knowledge in Life and Society.* Ann Arbor: University of Michigan Press, 1956.

Broadbent, Geoffrey; Bunt, Richard; and Jencks, Charles, eds. *Signs, Symbols, and Architecture*. New York: John Wiley, 1980.

Broadbent, Geoffrey, et al., eds. *Meaning and Behavior in the Built Environment*. New York: Wiley Interscience, 1980.

Brunk, H. D. *An Introduction to Mathematical Statistics*, 2nd ed. Lexington, Mass.: Xerox College Publishing, 1975.

Carter, Ernestine. *The Changing World of Fashion*. New York: Putnam's, 1977.

Casey, John and Scruton, Roger. "Modern Charlatanism III: Frozen Labyrinths: Roland Barthes." *The Cambridge Review* 98 (1976):87-93.

Cassirer, Ernst. *The Philosophy of Symbolic Forms*. Vol. I: *Language*. New Haven, Conn.: Yale University Press, 1955.

Chafe, Wallace L. *Meaning and the Structure of Language*. Chicago: University of Chicago Press, 1970.

Chapman, Dennis. *The Home and Social Status*. London: Routledge and Kegan Paul, 1955.

Chatman, Seymour; Eco, Umberto; and Klinkenberg, Jean-Marie, eds. *A Semiotic Landscape*, Proceedings of the First Congress of the International Association for Semiotic Studies, Milan, June 1974. The Hague: Mouton Publishers, 1979.

Cherry, Colin. *On Human Communication*. *A Review, a Survey, and a Criticism*. 2nd ed. Cambridge, Mass.: MIT Press, 1957.

Chicago Magazine. April, May, June, and July, 1981. Chicago: WFMT, Inc.

Chomsky, Noam. *Aspects of the Theory of Syntax*. Cambridge, Mass.: MIT Press, 1965.

_____. "Deep Structure, Surface Structure, and Semantic Interpretation." In *Studies in General and Oriental Linguistics, Presented to Shiro Hattori on the Occasion of his Sixtieth Birthday*. Edited by Roman Jakobson and Shigeo Kanamoto. Tokyo: TEC Co., 1970.

_____. *Language and Mind*. enlarged ed. New York: Harcourt, Brace, Jovanovich, Inc., 1968.

_____. *Reflections on Language*. New York: Pantheon Books, 1975.

Clay, Grady. *Close-Up: How to Read the American City*. Chicago: University of Chicago Press, 1980.

Cohen, Abner. "Political Anthropology: The Analysis of the Symbolism of Power Relations." *Man* 4 (1969):215-235.

_____. *Two-Dimensional Man: An Essay on the Anthropology of Power and Symbolism in Complex Society*. Berkeley: University of California Press, 1974.

Congress of the International Colour Association. *Colour 73*, Survey Lectures and Abstracts of the Papers Presented at the Second Congress of the International Colour Association, The University of York, 2-6 July 1973. New York: John Wiley and Sons, 1973.

Coward, Rosalind and Ellis, John. *Language and Materialism*. *Developments in Semiology and the Theory of the Subject*. London: Routledge and Kegan Paul, 1977.

Craig, Lois and the staff of The Federal Architecture Project. *The Federal Presence: Architecture, Politics, and Symbols in United States Government Building*. Cambridge, Mass.: MIT Press, 1978.

Crane, David A. "The City Symbolic." *AIP Journal* 26 (1960):280-292.

Csikszentmihalyi, Mihaly and Rochberg-Halton, Eugene. *The Meaning of Things: Domestic Symbols and the Self*. New York: Cambridge University Press, 1981.

Davis, James A. "Living Rooms as Symbols of Social Status: A Study in Social Judgment." Ph.D. Dissertation, Harvard University, 1955.

Dittmar, Norbert. *A Critical Survey of Sociolinguistics: Theory and Application*. New York: St. Martin's Press, 1976.

Ditton, Jason, ed. *The View from Goffman*. New York: St. Martin's, 1980.

Douglas, Mary. *Natural Symbols*. New York: Pantheon Books, 1970.

Downs, Roger M. and Stea, David, eds. *Image and Environment*. *Cognitive Mapping and Spatial Behavior*. Chicago: Aldine Publishing Company, 1973.

Duncan, Hugh Dalziel. *Communication and Social Order*. New York: Oxford University Press, 1962.

____. *Symbols and Social Theory*. New York: Oxford University Press, 1969.

____. *Symbols in Society*. New York: Oxford University Press, 1968.

Duncan, James S., Jr. "Landscape and the Communication of Social Identity." In *The Mutual Interaction of People and Their Built Environment: A Cross-Cultural Perspective*, pp. 391-401. Edited by Amos Rapoport. The Hague: Mouton Publishers, 1976.

Duttmann, Martina; Schmuck, Friedrich; and Uhl, Johannes. *Color in Townscape*. San Francisco: W. H. Freeman and Co., 1981.

Eco, Umberto. "A Componential Analysis of the Architectural Sign /Column/." In *Signs, Symbols, and Architecture*, pp. 213-232. Edited by Geoffrey Broadbent, Richard Bunt, and Charles Jencks. New York: John Wiley, 1980.

____. *A Theory of Semiotics*. Bloomington: Indiana University Press, 1976.

____. "Function and Sign: The Semiotics of Architecture." In *Signs, Symbols, and Architecture*, pp. 11-79. Edited by Geoffrey Broadbent, Richard Bunt, and Charles Jencks. New York: John Wiley, 1980.

Erickson, E. Gordon. *The Territorial Experience: Human Ecology as Symbolic Interaction*. Foreword by Herbert Blumer. Austin: University of Texas Press, 1980.

Faulkner, Waldron. *Architecture and Color*. New York: Wiley Interscience, 1972.

Fauve, Jean-Paul and November, Andre. *Color and Communication*. Zurich, Switzerland: ABC Editions, 1979.

Ferguson, George. *Signs and Symbols in Christian Art*. New York: Oxford University Press, 1981.

Firth, Raymond. *Symbols: Public and Private*. Ithaca, N.Y.: Cornell University Press, 1973.

Foucault, Michel. *The Archaeology of Knowledge*. London: Tavistock Publications, 1972.

____. *Language, Counter-Memory, Practice: Selected Essays and Interviews*. Ithaca, N.Y.: Cornell University Press, 1977.

____. *The Order of Things: An Archaeology of the Human Sciences*. New York: Pantheon Books, 1970.

____. *Power/Knowledge: Selected Interviews and Other Writings, 1972-1977*. New York: Pantheon Books, 1980.

Gandelsonas, Mario. "From Structure to Subject: The Formation of an Architectural Language." *Oppositions* 17 (Summer 1979):6-29.

____. "Linguistics, Poetics and Architectural Theory." *Semiotexte* 1 (Fall 1974):88-94.

Gatto, Joseph A. *Color and Value: Design Elements*. Worcester, Mass.: Davis Mass, 1974.

Gatz, Konrad and Wallenfang, Wilhelm O. *Color in Architecture: A Guide to Exterior Design*. New York: Reinhold Publishing Corporation, 1961.

Gavel, Jonas. *Colour: A Study of its Position in the Art Theory of the Quattro- and Cinquecento*. Stockholm, Sweden: Alquist and Wiksell International, 1979.

Geertz, Clifford. *The Interpretation of Cultures*. New York: Basic Books, 1973.

Ghioca, Gabriela. "A Comparative Analysis of Architectural Signs (Applied to Columns)." *Semiotica* 14 (1975):40-51.

Glacken, Clarence J. *Traces on the Rhodian Shore: Nature and Culture in Western Thought from Ancient Times to the End of the Eighteenth Century*. Berkeley: University of California Press, 1967.

Goffman, Erving. *Behavior in Public Places. Notes on the Social Organization of Gatherings*. New York: Free Press, 1963.

____. *The Presentation of Self in Everyday Life*. Garden City, N.Y.: Doubleday, 1959.

____. *Strategic Interaction*. Philadelphia: University of Pennsylvania Press, 1969.

Goodman, Nelson. *Languages of Art: An Approach to a Theory of Symbols*. 2nd ed. Indianapolis: Hackett Publishing Co., 1976.

Greenbie, Barrie B. *Spaces: Dimensions of the Human Landscape*. New Haven, Conn.: Yale University Press, 1981.

Gregory, Michael and Carroll, Susanne. *Language and Situation*. London: Routledge and Kegan Paul, 1978.

Guillerme, Jacques. "The Idea of Architectural Language: A Critical Review." *Oppositions* 10 (Fall 1977):21-26.

Guiraud, Pierre. *Semiology*. London: Routledge and Kegan Paul, 1975.

Harris, Roy. *The Language Myth*. New York: St. Martin's, 1981.

_____. *Synonymy and Linguistic Analysis*. Toronto: University of Toronto Press, 1973.

Hawkes, Terence. *Structuralism and Semiotics*. Berkeley: University of California Press, 1977.

Hayakawa, S. I. *Symbols, Status, and Personality*. New York: Harcourt, Brace, and World, 1953.

Hebdige, Dick. *Subculture: The Meaning of Style*. New York: Methuen, Inc., 1979.

Heckscher, August (with Robinson, Phyllis). *Open Spaces: The Life of American Cities*. New York: Harper and Row Publishers, 1977.

Hjelmslev, Louis. *Language*. Madison: University of Wisconsin Press, 1970.

Hudson, R. A. *Sociolinguistics*. New York: Cambridge University Press, 1980.

Hymes, Dell. *Foundations in Sociolinguistics: An Ethnographic Approach*. Philadelphia: University of Pennsylvania Press, 1974.

Illinois Hotel and Motel Association. *Illinois Hotel/Motel Directory, 1981-1982*. Springfield: State of Illinois, The Office of Tourism, Department of Commerce and Community Affairs, 1981.

International Encyclopedia of the Social Sciences. 1968 ed. S.v. "Landscape," by Marvin W. Mikesell.

Jackson, J. B. *The Necessity for Ruins, and other Topics*. Amherst: University of Massachusetts Press, 1980.

Jakobson, Roman. *The Framework of Language*. Michigan Studies in the Humanities, no. 1. Ann Arbor: University of Michigan, Horace H. Rackham School of Graduate Studies, 1980.

_____. "Linguistics and Poetics." In *Style in Language*, pp. 350-377. Edited by Thomas Sebeok. Bloomington: Indiana University Press, 1960.

Jencks, Charles and Baird, George, eds. *Meaning in Architecture*. New York: George Braziller, 1966.

Kaplan, Sherman. *Best Restaurants: Chicago and Suburbs*. revised and expanded ed. San Francisco: 101 Publications, 1979.

Kemper, Rachel H. *Costume*. New York: Newsweek Books, 1977.

Kepes, Gyorgy. "Notes on Expression and Communication in the Cityscape." In *The Future Metropolis*, pp. 190-213. Edited by Lloyd Rodwin. New York: George Braziller, 1961.

_____, ed. *Sign, Image, Symbol*. New York: George Braziller, 1966.

Key Magazine. Weekly issues from June and July, 1981. Chicago: This Week in Chicago, Inc.

King, Anthony D., ed. *Buildings and Society: Essays on the Social Development o the Built Environment*. London: Routledge and Kegan Paul, 1980.

Krampen, Martin. *Meaning in the Urban Environment*. London: Pion Ltd., 1979.

Krier, Rob. *Urban Space*. New York: Rizzoli Publishers, 1979.

Labov, William. *Language in the Inner City: Studies in the Black English Vernacular*. Philadelphia: University of Pennsylvania Press, 1972.

_____. *Sociolinguistic Patterns*. Philadelphia: University of Pennsylvania Press, 1972.

Lakoff, George and Johnson, Mark. *Metaphors We Live By*. Chicago: University of Chicago Press, 1980.

Lamb, Sydney M. *Outline of Stratificational Grammar*. Washington, D.C.: Georgetown University Press, 1966.

Langer, Suzanne. *Philosophy in a New Key: A Study in the Symbolism of Reason, Rite, and Art*. 3rd. ed. Cambridge: Harvard University Press, 1957.

_____. *Feeling and Form: A Theory of Art Developed from Philosophy in a New Key*. New York: Charles Scribner's Sons, 1953.

Laurence, Frederick S. *Color in Architecture*. New York: National Terra Cotta Society, 1924.

Laver, James. *The Concise History of Costume and Fashion*. New York: Abrams, 1969.

Leach, Edmund. *Culture and Communication: The Logic by which Symbols are Connected. An Introduction to the use of Structuralist Analysis in Social Anthropology*. Cambridge: Cambridge University Press, 1976.

Lehmann, Erich L. and Tanur, Judith., eds. *Statistics: A Guide to the Unknown*, 2nd ed. San Francisco: Holden-Day, 1972.

Lenihan, John and Fletcher, William. *Environment and Man*. Vol. 8: *The Built Environment*. New York: Academic Press, 1979.

Libby, William Charles. *Color and the Structural Sense*. Englewood Cliffs, N.J.: Prentice-Hall, Inc., 1974.

Lurie, Alison. *The Language of Clothes*. New York: Random House, 1981.

Lynch, Kevin. *The Image of the City*. Cambridge, Mass.: MIT Press, 1960.

Lyons, John. *Introduction to Theoretical Linguistics*. Cambridge: Cambridge University Press, 1969.

Markuzon, V. "An Attempt to Redefine the 'Language of Architecture' in Terms of Semantics." *Architectural Association Quarterly* 4(1972):41-48.

Matejka, Ladislav and Titunik, Irwin R. *Semiotics of Art: Prague School Contributions*. Cambridge, Mass.: MIT Press, 1976.

McFall, Sherry, ed. *Chicago Banks: Directory of Officers and Financial Statements and Suburban Cook County Bank Officers*. Chicago: Law Bulletin Publishing, Co., January 1981.

Meier, Richard L. *A Communications Theory of Urban Growth*. Cambridge, Mass.: MIT Press, 1962.

Meinig, Donald W., ed. *The Interpretation of Ordinary Landscapes: Geographical Essays*. New York: Oxford University Press, 1979.

Meltzer, Bernard N.; Petras, John W.; and Reynolds, Larry T. *Symbolic Interactonism: Genesis, Varieties, and Criticism*. London: Routledge and Kegan Paul, 1975.

Miller, Nory. "The Re-Emergence of Color as a Design Tool." *American Institute of Architects Journal* 67 (October 1978):40-55.

Mitchell, W. J. T., ed. *The Language of Images*. Chicago: University of Chicago Press, 1974.

Moles, Abraham. "Objet et communication." *Communications* 13 (1969):1-21.

Morris, Charles. *Signs, Language, and Behavior*. New York: Prentice-Hall, 1946.

Mukarovsky, Jan. *Structure, Sign, and Function. Selected Essays by Jan Mukarovsky*. Translated and edited by John Burbank and Peter Steiner. New Haven, Conn.: Yale University Press, 1978.

Munsell, Albert H. *A Color Notation*. 13th ed. Baltimore, Md.: Munsell Color Co., 1979.

Needham, Rodney. *Reconnaissances*. Toronto: University of Toronto Press, 1980.

_____. *Symbolic Classification*. Santa Monica, Cal.: Goodyear Publishing, 1979.

Nickerson, Dorothy. "History of the Munsell Color System, Company, and Foundation: Part I." *Color Research and Application* 1 (Spring 1976):7-10; and "History of the Munsell Color System, Company, and Foundation: Part II." *Color Research and Application* 1 (Summer 1976):69-77.

148

Norberg-Schulz, Christian. "Kahn, Heidegger and the Language of Architecture." *Oppositions* 18 (Fall 1979):28-47.

Ogden, C. K. and Richards, I. A. *The Meaning of Meaning: A Study of the Influence of Language upon Thought and of the Science of Symbolism*. New York: Harcourt, Brace, and World, Inc., 1923.

Ortony, Andrew, ed. *Metaphor and Thought*. Cambridge: Cambridge University Press, 1979.

Panofsky, Erwin. *Meaning in the Visual Arts*. Garden City, N.J.: Doubleday and Company, 1955.

Pavey, Donald. *Color*. Los Angeles: Knapp Press, 1980.

Peirce, Charles Santiago Sanders. *Collected Papers*. Edited by Charles Hartshorne and Paul Weiss. Cambridge: Harvard University Press, 1931-1958.

Pevsner, Nikolaus. *A History of Building Types*. Princeton, N.J.: Princeton University Press, 1976.

Piaget, Jean. *Structuralism*. Translated and edited by Chaninah Maschler. New York: Harper and Row, 1970.

Polhemus, Ted and Proctor, Lynn. *Fashion and Anti-Fashion: Anthropology of Clothing and Adornment*. London: Thames and Hudson, 1978.

Pons, Valdo. *Imagery and Symbolism in Urban Society*. Hull, England: Published for the University of Hull by Lowgate Press, 1975.

Porter, Tom and Milellides, Byron. *Color for Architecture*. New York: Van Nostrand Reinhold, 1976.

Preziosi, Donald. *Architecture, Language, and Meaning*. The Hague: Mouton Publishers, 1979.

____. *The Semiotics of the Built Environment: An Introduction to Architectonic Analysis*. Bloomington: Indiana University Press, 1979.

Price, J. B. and Holmes, Janet, eds. *Sociolinguistics*. New York: Penguin, 1972.

Prieto, Luis J. *Messages et Signaux*. Paris: Presses Universitaires de France, 1966.

Rand McNally and Co. *Mobil Travel Guide: Great Lakes Area, 1981*. Chicago: Rand McNally and Co., 1981.

Rapoport, Amos. *House Form and Culture*. Englewood Cliffs, N.J.: Prentice-Hall, Inc., 1969.

____. *The Meaning of the Built Environment: A Non-Verbal Communication Approach*. Beverly Hills, Cal.: Sage, 1982.

____. "On the Environment and the Definition of the Situation." *International Architect* 1 (1979):26-29.

Rasmussen, David M. *Symbol and Interpretation*. The Hague: Martinus Hijhoff, 1974.

Reddy, Michael J. "The Conduit Metaphor." In *Metaphor and Thought,* pp. 284-324. Edited by Andrew Ortony. Cambridge: Cambridge University Press, 1979.

Richards, I. A. *Complementarities: Uncollected Essays*. Edited by John Paul Russo. Cambridge: Harvard University Press, 1976.

____. *The Philosophy of Rhetoric*. New York: Oxford University Press, 1936.

Richardson, Miles, ed. *The Human Mirror: Material and Spatial Images of Man*. Baton Rouge: Louisiana State University Press, 1974.

Ricoeur, Paul. *The Rule of Metaphor: Multi-disciplinary Studies of the Creation of Meaning in Language*. Translated by Robert Czerny. Toronto: University of Toronto Press, 1977.

Rock, Irvin. *An Introduction to Perception*. New York: Macmillan, 1975.

Ruesch, Jurgen, ed. *Semiotic Approaches to Human Relations*. The Hague: Mouton, 1972.

Saarinen, Thomas F. *Environmental Planning: Perception and Behavior*. Boston: Houghton-Mifflin Company, 1976.

Sacks, Sheldon, ed. Special Issue on Metaphor. *Critical Inquiry*. 5 (Autumn 1978). Republished as *On Metaphor*. Edited by Sheldon Sacks. Chicago: University of Chicago Press, 1979.

149

Sankoff, Gillian. *The Social Life of Language.* Philadelphia: University of
Pennsylvania Press, 1980.

Sapir, J. David, and Crocker, Christopher J. *The Social Use of Metaphor: Essays
on the Anthropology of Rhetoric.* Philadelphia: University of Pennsylvania
Press, 1977.

Saussure, Ferdinand de. *Course in General Linguistics.* Translated by Wade
Baskin. New York: McGraw-Hill Co., 1959.

Scherer, Klaus R. and Giles, Howard. *Social Markers in Speech.* Cambridge:
Cambridge University Press, 1979.

Schlereth, Thomas J. "The City as Artifact." *Newsletter* of the American History
Society (February 1977):6-9.

Schofer, Peter and Rice, Donald. "Metaphor, Metonymy, and Synecdoche
Revis(it)ed." *Semiotica* 21 (1977):121-144.

Scruton, Roger. *The Aesthetics of Architecture.* Princeton, N.J.: Princeton
University Press, 1979.

Searle, John R. *Speech Acts: An Essay in the Philosophy of Language.* Cambridge:
Cambridge University Press, 1969.

Sebeok, Thomas A., ed. *A Perfusion of Signs.* Bloomington: Indiana University
Press, 1977.

Sebeok, Thomas A.; Hayes, A. S.; and Bateson, M. C., eds. *Approaches to
Semiotics.* The Hague: Mouton, 1964.

Sheridan, Alan. *Michel Foucault: The Will to Truth.* London and New York:
Tavistock Publications, 1980.

Sims, John H. and Baumann, Duane D., eds. *Human Behavior and the Environment:
Interactions Between Man and His Physical World.* Chicago: Maaroufa Press,
1974.

Singer, Milton. "Emblems of Identity: A Semiotic Exploration." In *Symbols in
Anthropology,* pp. 73-133. Edited by J. Maquet. Malibu, Cal.: Undena
Publications, 1982.

_____. "For a Semiotic Anthropology." In *Sight, Sound, and Sense,* pp.
202-231. Edited by Thomas A. Sebeok. Bloomington: Indiana University
Press, 1978.

_____. "On the Semiotics of Indian Identity." *American Journal of Semiotics*
1 (1981):85-126.

_____. "On the Symbolic and Historic Structure of an American Identity."
Ethos 5 (1977):431-454.

_____. "Signs of the Self: An Exploration in Semiotic Anthropology."
American Anthropologist 82 (September 1980):485-507.

Sloane, Patricia. *Colour: Basic Principles, New Directions.* New York: Reinhold
Book Corp, 1967.

Smith, Earl Baldwin. *Architectural Symbolism of Imperial Rome and the Middle
Ages.* Princeton, N.J.: Princeton University Press, 1956.

_____. *Egyptian Architecture as Cultural Expression.* New York: D. Appleton-
Century Co., 1938.

Smithson, Alison and Smithson, Peter. *Without Rhetoric: An Architectural
Aesthetic 1955-1972.* Cambridge, Mass.: MIT Press, 1973.

Specter, David Kenneth. *Urban Spaces.* Greenwich, Conn.: New York Graphic
Society, 1974.

Sperber, Dan. *Rethinking Symbolism.* Translated by Alice L. Morton. Cambridge:
Cambridge University Press, 1975.

Squires, Geoffrey. *Dress and Society, 1560-1970.* New York: Viking, 1974.

Steiner, George. *After Babel. Aspects of Language and Translation.* New York:
Oxford University Press, 1975.

Stone, Gregory P. "Clothing and Social Relations: A Study of Appearance in the
Context of Community Life." Ph.D. Dissertation, The University of Chicago,
Department of Sociology, 1959.

Strauss, Anselm L. *Images of the American City.* New York: Free Press of
Glencoe, 1961.

Stryker, Sheldon. *Symbolic Interactionism: A Social Structural Version.* Menlo Park, Cal.: Benjamin/Cummings, 1980.

Tafuri, Manfredo. *Architecture and Utopia: Design and Capitalist Development.* Translated by Barbara Luigia La Penta. Cambridge, Mass.: MIT Press, 1976.

_____. *Theories and History of Architecture.* Translated by Giorgio Verrecchia. New York: Harper & Row, Publishers, 1980.

Taylor, Lisa. ed. *Urban Open Spaces.* New York: Rizzoli International, 1981.

Toyama, Tomonori. "A Semiotic Analysis of Semiotic Approaches to Architecture." *Semiosis 14: Zietschrift fur Semiotik und ihre Anwendungen* 2 (1979):26-33.

Tuan, Yi-Fu. "Sign and Metaphor." *Annals of the Association of American Geographers* 68 (September 1978):363-372.

_____. *Topophilia. A Study of Environmental Perception, Attitudes, and Values.* Englewood Cliffs, N.J.: Prentice-Hall, Inc., 1974.

Turner, Victor. *Dramas, Fields, and Metaphors: Symbolic Action in Human Society.* Ithaca, N.Y.: Cornell University Press, 1974.

U.S. Department of Commerce. National Bureau of Standards. *Color: Universal Language and Dictionary of Names,* by Kenneth L. Kelly and Deane B. Judd. Washington, D.C.: Government Printing Office, 1976.

Van Zanten, David. *Architectural Polychromy of the 1830's.* New York: Garland Publishing, Inc., 1977.

Veblen, Thorstein. *The Theory of the Leisure Class: An Economic Study of the Evolution of Institutions.* New York: MacMillan and Co., 1955.

Venturi, Robert; Brown, Denise Scott; and Izenour, Steven. *Learning from Las Vegas: The Forgotten Symbolism of Architectural Form.* Cambridge, Mass.: MIT Press, 1972.

Wagner, Philip L. "Cultural Landscapes and Regions: Aspects of Communication." *Geoscience and Man* 5 (1974):133-142.

_____. *Environments and Peoples.* Englewood Cliffs, N.J.: Prentice-Hall, Inc., 1972.

Wallis, Mieczyslaw. *Arts and Signs.* Indiana University Publications, Studies in Semiotics, vol. 2. Bloomington: Indiana University Publications, Studies in Semiotics, 1975.

_____. "Semantic and Symbolic Elements in Architecture: Iconology as a First Step Towards an Architectural Semiotic." *Semiotica* 8 (1973):220-238.

Where Magazine: Chicago. Weekly issues from June and July, 1981. Chicago: Media Networks, Inc.

Wheatley, Paul. *City as Symbol,* An inaugural lecture delivered at University College, London, 20 November, 1967. London: Published for the College by H. K. Lewis, 1969.

Whorf, Benjamin Lee. *Language, Thought, and Reality. Selected Writings of Benjamin Lee Whorf.* Edited by John B. Carroll. Cambridge, Mass.: MIT Press, 1956.

Wittgenstein, Ludwig. *Remarks on Colour.* Berkeley: University of California Press, 1977.

Wohl, R. R. and Strauss, A. "Symbolic Representation and the Urban Milieu." *American Journal of Sociology* 63 (March 1958):523-532.

Yarwood, Doreen. *The Encyclopedia of World Costume.* New York: Scribners, 1978.

Yngve, Victor H. "The Dilemma of Contemporary Linguistics." In *The First Lacus Forum, 1974.* Edited by Adam Makkai and Valerie Becker Makkai. Columbia, S.C.: Hornbeam Press, 1975.

_____. *Human Linguistics: The Scientific Study of How People Communicate.* Unpublished Manuscript, University of Chicago, Revised 1980.

_____. "On Achieving Agreement in Linguistics." In *Papers from the Fifth Regional Meeting of the Chicago Linguistics Society, April 18-19, 1969.* Edited by Robert I. Binnick, Alice Davison, Georgia M Green, and Jerry L. Morgan. Chicago: University of Chicago, Department of Linguistics, 1969.

_____. "Stoic Influences in Librarianship: A Critique." In *Libraries and Culture,* Proceedings of Library History Seminar VI, 19-22 March 1980, pp. 92-105. Edited by Donald G. Davis. Austin: University of Texas Press, 1981.

151

_____. "The Struggle for a Theory of Native Speaker." In *A Festschrift for Native Speaker,* pp. 29-49. Edited by Florian Coulmas. The Hague: Mouton, 1981.

_____. "Toward a Human Linguistics." In *Papers from the Parasession on Functionalism, Chicago Linguistics Society, April 17, 1975.* Edited by Robin E. Grossman, L. James San, and Timothy J. Vance. Chicago: Chicago Linguistics Society, University of Chicago, Department of Linguistics, 1975.

SUPPLEMENTARY SOURCES

In addition to the works listed above, all of which have been cited in preceding footnotes, the following books and articles represent the traditions of investigation which have combined to inspire the present study and which, it is hoped, will be influenced by it. Although no distinctions are made within the alphabetical listing, the works are drawn from the literatures of (1) architectural design, theory, and criticism; (2) the behavioral sciences; (3) culture history and art history; (4) religious studies; (5) semiotics and the communicational sciences; (6) social, cultural, and political anthropology; (7) social, cultural, and behavioral geography; (8) sociology (including studies in symbolic interactionism); and (9) the study of political institutions.

Alexander, Christopher; Ishikawa, Sara; and Silverstein, Murray. *A Pattern Language.* New York: Oxford University Press, 1977.

Barker, Roger G. *Ecological Psychology: Concepts and Methods for Studying the Environment of Human Behavior.* Stanford, Cal.: Stanford University Press, 1968.

Bastian, Robert W. "Architecture and Class Segregation in Late Nineteenth-Century Terre Haute, Indiana." *The Geographical Review* 65 (April 1975):166-179.

Becker, Franklin D. *Housing Messages.* Stroudsburg, Penn.: Dowden, Hutchinson & Ross, Co., 1977.

Bell, David V. J. *Power, Influence, and Authority. An Essay in Political Linguistics.* New York: Oxford University Press, 1975.

Birker, Erwin. *Urbildsprache altchristlicher Baukunst. Studien am Geprage d. altchristlichen Basilika im Vergleich mit der arabischen, romanischen und gotischen Baugestalt.* Stuttgart: Mellinger, 1967.

Bloomer, Kent C. and Moore, Charles W. *Body, Memory, and Architecture.* New Haven, Conn.: Yale University Press, 1977.

Brown, Donald N. "Social Structure as Reflected in Architectural Units at Picuris Pueblo." In *The Human Mirror: Material and Spatial Images of Man.* Edited by Miles Richardson. Baton Rouge: Louisiana State University Press, 1974.

Conzen, M.R.G. *The Urban Landscape: Historical Development and Management,* Papers by M.R.G. Conzen. Edited by J.W.R. Whitehand. London: Academic Press, 1981.

Cooper, Clare C. *Easter Hill Village: Some Social Implications of Design.* New York: The Free Press, 1975.

Crosby, Theo. *The Necessary Monument: Its Future in the Civilized City.* Greenwich, Conn.: New York Graphic Society, 1970.

_____. *Symbols and Social Theory.* New York: Oxford University Press, 1969.

Eickelman, Dale F. "Symbolic Form and Urban Social Space: A Moroccan Example." In *Systeme Urbain et Developement au Maghreb.* Edited by A. Zghal and A. Rassam. Tunis: Editions CERES-Productions, 1978.

Eliade, Mircea. *Images and Symbols: Studies in Religious Symbolism.* London: Harvill Press, 1961.

Eliade, Mircea. "Sacred Space and Making the World Sacred." In *The Sacred and the Profane,* pp. 20-65. New York: Harper Torchbooks, 1961.

Giedion, Sigfried. *Space, Time, and Architecture: The Growth of a New Tradition.* 5th ed. Cambridge.: Harvard University Press, 1967.

Gold, John R. *Communicating Images of the Environment,* University of Birmingham, Centre for Urban and Regional Studies, Occasional Paper, no. 29. Birmingham, England: University of Birmingham, Centre for Urban and Regional Studies, 1974.

Gold, John R. and Burgess, Jacquelin, eds. *Valued Environments*. Boston: Allen and Unwin, 1982.

Gutman, Robert. "The Social Function of the Built Environment." In *The Mutual Interaction of People and Their Built Environment: A Cross-Cultural Perspective,* pp. 37-49. Edited by Amos Rapoport. The Hague: Mouton Publishers, 1976.

Hall, Edward. "Environmental Communication." In *Behavior and Environment: The Use of Space by Animals and Men*. Edited by Aristide H. Esser. New York: Plenum Press, 1971.

Harvey, David. "Monument and Myth." *Annals of the Association of American Geographers* 69 (September 1979):362-381.

Hershberger, Robert G. "Architecture and Meaning." *Journal of Aesthetic Education* 4 (1970):37-55.

_____. "A Study of Meaning and Architecture." Ph.D. Dissertation, University of Pennsylvania, 1969.

Hodder, Ian. *Symbols in Action: Ethnoarchaeological Studies of Material Culture*. New York: Cambridge University Press, 1982.

Lasswell, Harold D. *The Signature of Power: Buildings, Communication, and Policy*. New Brunswick, N.J.: Transaction, Inc., 1979.

Lasswell, Harold D.; Leites, Nathan; and Associates. *Language of Politics. Studies in Quantitative Semantics*. Cambridge, Mass.: MIT Press, 1949.

Lethaby, William Richard. *Architecture, Mysticism, and Myth*. New York: George Braziller, 1975; reprint ed., London: Percival, 1891.

Lewis, Pierce F. "Axioms for Reading the Landscape: Some Guides to the American Scene." In *The Interpretation or Ordinary Landscapes*. Edited by D. W. Meinig. New York: Oxford University Press, 1979.

Ley, David and Samuels, Marwyn S., eds. *Humanistic Geography: Prospects and Problems*. Chicago: Maaroufa Press, 1978.

Lowenthal, David. "Past Time, Present Place: Landscape and Memory." *The Geographical Review* 65 (January 1975):1-36.

_____, ed. *Environmental Perception and Behavior*. University of Chicago, Department of Geography Research Papers, no. 109. Chicago: University of Chicago, Department of Geography, 1967.

Lowenthal, David and Bowden, Martyn, eds. *Geographies of the Mind: Essays in Historical Geosophy in Honor of John Kirtland Wright*. New York: Oxford University Press, 1976.

Marc, Olivier. *The Psychology of the House*. London: Thames and Hudson, 1977.

Merritt, Richard L. *Symbols of American Community, 1735-1775*. New Haven: Yale University Press, 1966.

Muller, Werner. *Die heilige Stadt: Roma quadrata, himmlishes Jerusalem und die Myth vom Weltnabel*. Stuttgart: W. Kohlhammer, 1961.

Mumford, Lewis. *Sticks and Stones: A Study of American Architecture and Civilization*. 2nd ed. New York: Dover, 1955.

Newton, Milton B., Jr. "Settlement Patterns as Artifacts of Social Structure." In *The Human Mirror: Material and Spatial Images of Man*. Edited by Miles Richardson. Baton Rouge: Louisiana State University Press, 1974.

Norberg-Schulz, Christian. *Intentions in Architecture*. Cambridge, Mass.: MIT Press, 1965.

Oliver, Paul, ed. *Shelter, Sign and Symbol*. Woodstock, N.Y.: Overlook Press, 1977.

Pile, John F. *Design: Purpose, Form, and Meaning*. Amherst: University of Massachusetts Press, 1979.

Porteus, John D. "Home: The Territorial Core." *The Geographical Review* 66 (October 1976):383-390.

Prak, Niels Luning. *The Language of Architecture: A Contribution to Architectural Theory*. The Hague: Mouton, 1968.

Quimby, Ian M. G., ed. *Material Culture and the Study of American Life*. The 21st Winterthur Conference. New York: Norton for the Winterthur Museum, Winterthur, Delaware, 1975.

Raglan, Lord. *The Temple and the House*. London: Routledge and Kegan Paul, 1964.

Rapoport, Amos, ed. *Human Aspects of Urban Form: Towards a Man-Environment Approach to Urban Form and Design*. New York: Pergamon Press, 1977.

Rasmussen, Steen Eiler. *Experiencing Architecture*. Cambridge, Mass.: MIT Press, 1962.

Relph, E. C. *Place and Placelessness*. London: Pion Ltd., 1976.

Rochberg-Halton, Eugene. "Cultural Signs and Urban Adaptation: The Meaning of Cherished Household Possessions." Ph.D. Dissertation, University of Chicago, Department of Behavioral Sciences, 1979.

_____. "On the Use of Personal Objects as Symbols." Unpublished Research Paper, University of Chicago, Department of Behavioral Sciences, Committee on Human Development, August 1976.

_____. "A Preliminary Investigation of Urban Cultural Symbols in Chicago." Unpublished Research Paper, University of Chicago, Department of Behavioral Sciences, Committee on Human Development, December 1976.

Rowntree, Lester B. and Conkey, Margaret W. "Symbolism and the Cultural Landscape." *Annals of the Association of American Geographers* 70 (December 1980):459-474.

Samuels, Marwyn S. "The Biography of Landscape: Cause and Culpability." In *The Interpretation of Ordinary Landscapes*, pp. 51-88. Edited by D. W. Meinig. New York: Oxford University Press, 1979.

Smith, Earl Baldwin. *Architectural Symbolism of Imperial Rome and the Middle Ages*. Princeton, N.J.: Princeton University Press, 1956.

_____. *Egyptian Architecture as Cultural Expression*. New York: D. Appleton-Century Co., 1938.

Smithson, Alison and Smithson, Peter. *Without Rhetoric: An Architectural Aesthetic 1955-1972*. Cambridge, Mass.: MIT Press, 1973.

Sommer, Robert. *Personal Space: The Behavioral Basis of Design*. Englewood Cliffs, N.J.: Prentice-Hall, 1969.

Strauss, Anselm L., ed. *The American City: A Sourcebook of Urban Imagery*. Chicago: Aldine Publishing Co., 1968.

Summerson, John. *The Classical Language of Architecture*. Cambridge, Mass.: MIT Press, 1963.

_____. *Heavenly Mansions, and other Essays on Architecture*. New York: Scribner, 1950.

Suttles, Gerald D. *The Social Construction of Communities*. Chicago: University of Chicago Press, 1972.

_____. *The Social Order of the Slum: Ethnicity and Territory in the Inner City*. Chicago: University of Chicago Press, 1968.

Taylor, Robert R. *The Word in Stone. The Role of Architecture in the National Socialist Ideology*.

Tuan, Yi-Fu. "Geopiety: A Theme in Man's Attachment to Nature and to Place." In *Geographies of the Mind*, pp. 11-39. Edited by David Lowenthal and Martyn Bowden. New York: Oxford University Press, 1976.

_____. "Place: An Experiential Perspective." *The Geographical Review* 65 (April 1975):151-165.

_____. "Space and Place: A Humanistic Perspective." *Progress in Geography* 6 (1974):211-252.

_____. "Thought and Landscape: The Eye and the Mind's Eye." In *The Interpretation of Ordinary Landscapes*. Edited by D. W. Meinig. New York: Oxford University Press, 1979.

Turner, Victor. *Dramas, Fields, and Metaphors: Symbolic Action in Human Society*. Ithaca, N.Y.: Cornell University Press, 1974.

_____. *The Ritual Process: Stucture and Anti-Structure*. Ithaca, N.Y.: Cornell University Press, 1969.

Wallis, Mieczyslaw. "Semantic and Symbolic Elements in Architecture: Iconology as a First Step Towards an Architectural Semiotic." *Semiotica* 8 (1973):220-238.

Warner, William Lloyd. *The Living and the Dead: A Study of the Symbolic Life of Americans*. New Haven: Yale University Press, 1959.

THE UNIVERSITY OF CHICAGO
DEPARTMENT OF GEOGRAPHY
RESEARCH PAPERS (Lithographed, 6×9 inches)

Available from Department of Geography, The University of Chicago, 5828 S. University Avenue, Chicago, Illinois 60637, U.S.A. Price: $8.00 each; by series subscription, $6.00 each.

LIST OF TITLES IN PRINT

48. BOXER, BARUCH. *Israeli Shipping and Foreign Trade.* 1957. 162 p.
62. GINSBURG, NORTON, editor. *Essays on Geography and Economic Development.* 1960. 173 p.
71. GILBERT, EDMUND WILLIAM *The University Town in England and West Germany.* 1961. 79 p.
72. BOXER, BARUCH. *Ocean Shipping in the Evolution of Hong Kong.* 1961. 108 p.
91. HILL, A. DAVID. *The Changing Landscape of a Mexican Municipio, Villa Las Rosas, Chiapas.* 1964. 121 p.
101. RAY, D. MICHAEL. *Market Potential and Economic Shadow: A Quantitative Analysis of Industrial Location in Southern Ontario.* 1965. 164 p.
102. AHMAD, QAZI. *Indian Cities: Characteristics and Correlates.* 1965. 184 p.
103. BARNUM, H. GARDINER. *Market Centers and Hinterlands in Baden-Württemberg.* 1966. 172 p.
105. SEWELL, W. R. DERRICK, et al. *Human Dimensions of Weather Modification.* 1966. 423 p.
107. SOLZMAN, DAVID M. *Waterway Industrial Sites: A Chicago Case Study.* 1967. 138 p.
108. KASPERSON, ROGER E. *The Dodecanese: Diversity and Unity in Island Politics.* 1967. 184 p.
109. LOWENTHAL, DAVID, editor, *Environmental Perception and Behavior.* 1967. 88 p.
112. BOURNE, LARRY S. *Private Redevelopment of the Central City, Spatial Processes of Structural Change in the City of Toronto.* 1967. 199 p.
13. BRUSH, JOHN E., and GAUTHIER, HOWARD L., JR., *Service Centers and Consumer Trips: Studies on the Philadelphia Metropolitan Fringe.* 1968. 182 p.
14. CLARKSON, JAMES D., *The Cultural Ecology of a Chinese Village: Cameron Highlands, Malaysia.* 1968. 174 p.
15. BURTON, IAN, KATES, ROBERT W., and SNEAD, RODMAN E. *The Human Ecology of Coastal Flood Hazard in Megalopolis.* 1968. 196 p.
17. WONG, SHUE TUCK, *Perception of Choice and Factors Affecting Industrial Water Supply Decisions in Northeastern Illinois.* 1968. 93 p.
18. JOHNSON, DOUGLAS L. *The Nature of Nomadism: A Comparative Study of Pastoral Migrations in Southwestern Asia and Northern Africa.* 1969. 200 p.
19. DIENES, LESLIE. *Locational Factors and Locational Developments in the Soviet Chemical Industry.* 1969. 262 p.
20. MIHELIČ, DUŠAN. *The Political Element in the Port Geography of Trieste.* 1969. 104 p.
21. BAUMANN, DUANE D. *The Recreational Use of Domestic Water Supply Reservoirs: Perception and Choice.* 1969. 125 p.
22. LIND, AULIS O. *Coastal Landforms of Cat Island, Bahamas: A Study of Holocene Accretionary Topography and Sea-Level Change.* 1969. 156 p.
23. WHITNEY, JOSEPH B. R. *China: Area, Administration and Nation Building.* 1970. 198 p.
24. EARICKSON, ROBERT. *The Spatial Behavior of Hospital Patients: A Behavioral Approach to Spatial Interaction in Metropolitan Chicago.* 1970. 138 p.
25. DAY, JOHN CHADWICK. *Managing the Lower Rio Grande: An Experience in International River Development.* 1970. 274 p.
6. MacIVER, IAN. *Urban Water Supply Alternatives: Perception and Choice in the Grand Basin Ontario.* 1970. 178 p.
7. GOHEEN, PETER G. *Victorian Toronto, 1850 to 1900: Pattern and Process of Growth.* 1970. 278 p.
8. GOOD, CHARLES M. *Rural Markets and Trade in East Africa.* 1970. 252 p.
9. MEYER, DAVID R. *Spatial Variation of Black Urban Households.* 1970. 127 p.
0. GLADFELTER, BRUCE G. *Meseta and Campiña Landforms in Central Spain: A Geomorphology of the Alto Henares Basin.* 1971. 204 p.
1. NEILS, ELAINE M. *Reservation to City: Indian Migration and Federal Relocation.* 1971. 198 p.
2. MOLINE, NORMAN T. *Mobility and the Small Town, 1900–1930.* 1971. 169 p.
3. SCHWIND, PAUL J. *Migration and Regional Development in the United States.* 1971. 170 p.

134. PYLE, GERALD F. *Heart Disease, Cancer and Stroke in Chicago: A Geographical Analysis with Facilities, Plans for 1980.* 1971. 292 p.

135. JOHNSON, JAMES F. *Renovated Waste Water: An Alternative Source of Municipal Water Supply in the United States.* 1971. 155 p.

136. BUTZER, KARL W. *Recent History of an Ethiopian Delta: The Omo River and the Level of Lake Rudolf.* 1971. 184 p.

139. McMANIS, DOUGLAS R. *European Impressions of the New England Coast, 1497–1620.* 1972. 147 p.

140. COHEN, YEHOSHUA S. *Diffusion of an Innovation in an Urban System: The Spread of Planned Regional Shopping Centers in the United States, 1949–1968,* 1972. 136 p.

141. MITCHELL, NORA. *The Indian Hill-Station: Kodaikanal.* 1972. 199 p.

142. PLATT, RUTHERFORD H. *The Open Space Decision Process: Spatial Allocation of Costs and Benefits.* 1972. 189 p.

143. GOLANT, STEPHEN M. *The Residential Location and Spatial Behavior of the Elderly: A Canadian Example.* 1972. 226 p.

144. PANNELL, CLIFTON W. *T'ai-chung, T'ai-wan: Structure and Function.* 1973. 200 p.

145. LANKFORD, PHILIP M. *Regional Incomes in the United States, 1929–1967: Level, Distribution, Stability, and Growth.* 1972. 137 p.

146. FREEMAN, DONALD B. *International Trade, Migration, and Capital Flows: A Quantitative Analysis of Spatial Economic Interaction.* 1973. 201 p.

147. MYERS, SARAH K. *Language Shift Among Migrants to Lima, Peru.* 1973. 203 p.

148. JOHNSON, DOUGLAS L. *Jabal al-Akhdar, Cyrenaica: An Historical Geography of Settlement and Livelihood.* 1973. 240 p.

149. YEUNG, YUE-MAN. *National Development Policy and Urban Transformation in Singapore: A Study of Public Housing and the Marketing System.* 1973. 204 p.

150. HALL, FRED L. *Location Criteria for High Schools: Student Transportation and Racial Integration.* 1973. 156 p.

151. ROSENBERG, TERRY J. *Residence, Employment, and Mobility of Puerto Ricans in New York City.* 1974. 230 p.

152. MIKESELL, MARVIN W., editor. *Geographers Abroad: Essays on the Problems and Prospects of Research in Foreign Areas.* 1973. 296 p.

153. OSBORN, JAMES F. *Area, Development Policy, and the Middle City in Malaysia.* 1974. 291 p.

154. WACHT, WALTER F. *The Domestic Air Transportation Network of the United States.* 1974. 98 p.

155. BERRY, BRIAN J. L., *et al. Land Use, Urban Form and Environmental Quality.* 1974. 440 p.

156. MITCHELL, JAMES K. *Community Response to Coastal Erosion: Individual and Collective Adjustments to Hazard on the Atlantic Shore.* 1974. 209 p.

157. COOK, GILLIAN P. *Spatial Dynamics of Business Growth in the Witwatersrand.* 1975. 144 p.

159. PYLE, GERALD F. *et al. The Spatial Dynamics of Crime.* 1974. 221 p.

160. MEYER, JUDITH W. *Diffusion of an American Montessori Education.* 1975. 97 p.

161. SCHMID, JAMES A. *Urban Vegetation: A Review and Chicago Case Study.* 1975. 266 p.

162. LAMB, RICHARD F. *Metropolitan Impacts on Rural America.* 1975. 196 p.

163. FEDOR, THOMAS STANLEY. *Patterns of Urban Growth in the Russian Empire during the Nineteenth Century.* 1975. 245 p.

164. HARRIS, CHAUNCY D. *Guide to Geographical Bibliographies and Reference Works in Russian or on the Soviet Union.* 1975. 478 p.

165. JONES, DONALD W. *Migration and Urban Unemployment in Dualistic Economic Development* 1975. 174 p.

166. BEDNARZ, ROBERT S. *The Effect of Air Pollution on Property Value in Chicago.* 1975. 111 p.

167. HANNEMANN, MANFRED. *The Diffusion of the Reformation in Southwestern Germany, 1518–1534* 1975. 248 p.

168. SUBLETT, MICHAEL D. *Farmers on the Road. Interfarm Migration and the Farming of Noncontiguous Lands in Three Midwestern Townships, 1939-1969.* 1975. 228 pp.

169. STETZER, DONALD FOSTER. *Special Districts in Cook County: Toward a Geography of Local Government.* 1975. 189 pp.

170. EARLE, CARVILLE V. *The Evolution of a Tidewater Settlement System: All Hallow's Parish, Maryland, 1650–1783.* 1975. 249 pp.

171. SPODEK, HOWARD. *Urban-Rural Integration in Regional Development: A Case Study of Saurastra, India—1800-1960 .* 1976. 156 pp

172. COHEN, YEHOSHUA S. and BERRY, BRIAN J. L. *Spatial Components of Manufacturing Change.* 1975. 272 pp.

173. HAYES, CHARLES R. *The Dispersed City: The Case of Piedmont, North Carolina.* 1976. 169 pp.

174. CARGO, DOUGLAS B. *Solid Wastes: Factors Influencing Generation Rates.* 1977. 112 pp.

175. GILLARD, QUENTIN. *Incomes and Accessibility. Metropolitan Labor Force Participation, Commuting, and Income Differentials in the United States, 1960–1970.* 1977. 140 pp.

176. MORGAN, DAVID J. *Patterns of Population Distribution: A Residential Preference Model and Its Dynamic.* 1978. 216 pp.

177 STOKES, HOUSTON H.; JONES, DONALD W. and NEUBURGER, HUGH M. *Unemployment and Adjustment in the Labor Market: A Comparison between the Regional and National Responses.* 1975. 135 pp.

179. HARRIS, CHAUNCY D. *Bibliography of Geography. Part I. Introduction to General Aids.* 1976. 288 pp.

180. CARR, CLAUDIA J. *Pastoralism in Crisis. The Dasanetch and their Ethiopian Lands.* 1977. 339 pp.

181. GOODWIN, GARY C. *Cherokees in Transition: A Study of Changing Culture and Environment Prior to 1775.* 1977. 221 pp.

182. KNIGHT, DAVID B. *A Capital for Canada: Conflict and Compromise in the Nineteenth Century.* 1977. 359 pp.

183. HAIGH, MARTIN J. *The Evolution of Slopes on Artificial Landforms: Blaenavon, Gwent.* 1978. 311 pp.

184. FINK, L. DEE. *Listening to the Learner. An Exploratory Study of Personal Meaning in College Geography Courses.* 1977. 200 pp.

185. HELGREN, DAVID M. *Rivers of Diamonds: An Alluvial History of the Lower Vaal Basin.* 1979. 399 pp.

186. BUTZER, KARL W., editor. *Dimensions of Human Geography: Essays on Some Familiar and Neglected Themes.* 1978. 201 pp.

187. MITSUHASHI, SETSUKO. *Japanese Commodity Flows.* 1978. 185 pp.

188. CARIS, SUSAN L. *Community Attitudes toward Pollution.* 1978. 226 pp.

189. REES, PHILIP M. *Residential Patterns in American Cities, 1960.* 1979. 424 pp.

190. KANNE, EDWARD A. *Fresh Food for Nicosia.* 1979. 116 pp.

191. WIXMAN, RONALD. *Language Aspects of Ethnic Patterns and Processes in the North Caucasus.* 1980. 224 pp.

192. KIRCHNER, JOHN A. *Sugar and Seasonal Labor Migration: The Case of Tucumán, Argentina.* 1980. 158 pp.

193. HARRIS, CHAUNCY D. and FELLMANN, JEROME D. *International List of Geographical Serials, Third Edition, 1980.* 1980. 457 p.

194. HARRIS, CHAUNCY D. *Annotated World List of Selected Current Geographical Serials, Fourth Edition, 1980.* 1980. 165 p.

195. LEUNG, CHI-KEUNG. *China: Railway Patterns and National Goals.* 1980. 235 p.

196. LEUNG, CHI-KEUNG and NORTON S. GINSBURG, eds. *China: Urbanization and National Development.* 1980. 280 p.

197. DAICHES, SOL. *People in Distress: A Geographical Perspective on Psychological Well-being.* 1981. 199 p.

198. JOHNSON, JOSEPH T. *Location and Trade Theory: Industrial Location, Comparative Advantage, and the Geographic Pattern of Production in the United States.* 1981. 107 p.

199-200. STEVENSON, ARTHUR J. *The New York-Newark Air Freight System.* 1982. 440 p. (Double number, price: $16.00)

201. LICATE, JACK A. *Creation of a Mexican Landscape: Territorial Organization and Settlement in the Eastern Puebla Basin, 1520-1605.* 1981. 143 p.

202. RUDZITIS, GUNDARS. *Residential Location Determinants of the Older Population.* 1982. 117 p.

203. LIANG, ERNEST P. *China: Railways and Agricultural Development, 1875-1935.* 1982. 186 p.

204. DAHMANN, DONALD C. *Locals and Cosmopolitans: Patterns of Spatial Mobility during the Transition from Youth to Early Adulthood.* 1982. 146 p.

205. FOOTE, KENNETH E. *Color in Public Spaces: Toward a Communication-Based Theory of the Urban Built Environment.* 1983. 153 p.